EXPLORING GENDER IN VERNACULAR ARCHITECTURE

EXPLORING GENDER IN VERNACULAR ARCHITECTURE

Jessica Ellen Sewell

VERNACULAR ARCHITECTURE STUDIES

Thomas Carter and Anna Vemer Andrzejewski, *Series Editors*

The University of Tennessee Press / *Knoxville*

The Vernacular Architecture Studies series provides focused investigations into methodological and theoretical issues in the field of vernacular architecture studies. Written by experts in the field with the student, practitioner, and general public in mind, the series will comprise handbooks and historically grounded instructional texts that embody the very latest research from a burgeoning discipline in an accessible, practical form.

First Edition.

Library of Congress Cataloging-in-Publication Data

NAMES: Sewell, Jessica Ellen, author.

TITLE: Exploring gender in vernacular architecture / Jessica Ellen Sewell.

DESCRIPTION: First edition. | Knoxville : The University of Tennessee Press, [2025] SERIES: Vernacular architecture studies | Includes bibliographical references and index. |

SUMMARY: "In *Exploring Gender in Vernacular Architecture*, Jessica Ellen Sewell considers the gender of those who create and shape spaces, how gender ideology contributes to and manifests itself in built form, and what research methods make the observation of gendered experience possible. She discusses single-gender, mixed-gender, and queer spaces, providing a comprehensive look at how gender influences the design and construction of those spaces, how those spaces are used, and the relationship between gender and the broader architectural landscape"— Provided by publisher.

IDENTIFIERS: LCCN 2024041127 (print) | LCCN 2024041128 (ebook) | ISBN 9781621909316 (paperback) | ISBN 9781621909323 (adobe pdf) | ISBN 9781621909330 (kindle edition)

SUBJECTS: LCSH: Sex role in architecture. | Vernacular architecture. | Space (Architecture)—Psychological aspects.

CLASSIFICATION: LCC NA2543.S49 S49 2025 (print) | LCC NA2543.S49 (ebook) | DDC 720.81—dc23/eng/20240919

LC record available at https://lccn.loc.gov/2024041127

LC ebook record available at https://lccn.loc.gov/2024041128

For all the students of
my gender and the built
environment classes,
past, present, and future

Contents

Illustrations

Acknowledgments

This book grew from a firebrand of a paper I gave at the Vernacular Architecture Forum conference in Alexandria, Virginia, in 2018. My greatest thanks to Will Moore, who saw my presentation and thought "this should be a book." Tom Carter's belief in this book, his thoughtful feedback, and his work shepherding it through the process from a vague notion to the book in your hands has been invaluable. Many thanks to Scot Danforth, Jon Boggs, and their colleagues at the University of Tennessee Press for their support. Feedback from the VAF Special Series editorial board, anonymous readers, and Olivier Vallerand helped make this a stronger book than it would have been without them, and I thank them for their advice.

With support from the Vernacular Architecture Forum and the University of Virginia School of Architecture I was able to hire the student research assistants Zoha Kahn, Theodora Catrina, and Tabi Summers. A UVA Library research sprint with Rebecca Cooper Coleman, Erin Pappas, and Brandon Butler supercharged my image search. Off and on since 2001, I have been teaching a course on gender and the built environment. The students in these classes have taught me through their questions and their research and teaching them has pushed me to think critically about how we conceptualize gender.

Throughout the writing of this book, my husband Andy Johnston and son Ben Johnston have been my sounding board, my support team, and my covid isolation buddies. Special thanks to Ben, who was this book's first reader and who gave me some tips to improve my style.

1

THE PROBLEM OF GENDER IN VERNACULAR ARCHITECTURE

This book is a guide for those who are interested in the relationship between gender and the built environment: how the world of ordinary buildings and landscapes reflects and shapes ideas and experiences of what it is to be male, female, or non-binary within a culture. While the questions, methods, and case studies discussed here pertain to all aspects of the built environment, historical or contemporary, traditional or avant-garde, self-built or architect designed, this book is framed in the context of vernacular architecture studies. This is because vernacular architecture studies is grounded in the belief that buildings and landscapes express and embody culture, both ways of doing things and shared beliefs. The vernacular architecture studies approach to examining culture through the built environment makes it ideal for studying gender, since gender is a cultural and social category. This chapter explores these two concepts, vernacular architecture and gender, in more detail. It suggests how focusing on gender may transform and expand vernacular architecture scholarship and introduces how this book will guide you in your exploration of gender in vernacular architecture.

Vernacular Architecture

While what is meant by vernacular architecture has been much debated and has shifted over time, in the United States it is generally defined in two overlapping ways: by its object of study and by how it is practiced. The object of study in vernacular architecture studies is ordinary architecture, which can include handmade traditional buildings (the focus of British vernacular architecture studies), mass-culture buildings like strip malls and working-class bungalows, and even architect-designed buildings whose form or function is commonplace, such as dormitories and YMCAs. In addition to individual buildings, the field of vernacular architecture studies encompasses the cultural landscapes of which buildings are part and the material culture associated with them.[1] Defined as a kind of practice, methodologically and theoretically, vernacular architecture studies is an approach to architectural history that asks social and cultural questions and is based on the analysis of buildings and landscapes as artifacts.[2] The approach in this book starts from this definition, and examples include architect-designed, mass, and folk buildings, from a range of times and places.

Vernacular architecture studies came into its own as a field in the 1970s and early 1980s, in the context of a larger academic movement that focused on the lives and experiences of ordinary people, which included the new social history, labor history, ethnic studies, women's studies, and African American studies. This transformation of the study of history and society was tied to the social movements of the 1960s, which challenged dominant power structures, calling out White supremacy, sexism, colonialism, and corporate conformity. In this social and intellectual context, vernacular architecture studies is rooted in a broader impulse to tell a more complete story, one that focuses on ordinary people and common culture. Vernacular architecture studies was initially framed as a corrective to conventional architectural history, which addressed elite and unusual designs and focused on individual architects, rather than the social fabric of which they and the buildings they designed were a part.[3] Because of its desire for inclusivity and its historical roots in the social movements of the 1960s, vernacular architecture studies has always been deeply interested in questions of difference. The focus has been particularly on ethnic and regional difference as expressed in traditional modes of building and dwelling, but class, race, and gender have also been part of the discourse from the beginning.[4]

However, the theoretical and methodological roots of vernacular architecture studies have often hampered its ability to fully address questions of gender, as well as other aspects of difference within a culture or subculture. While vernacular architecture studies has always been interdisciplinary, it has particularly strong roots in the disciplines of historic preservation, folklore, art and architectural history, and the field of material culture studies, as well as in American studies and social history.[5] Theoretical assumptions about the unified nature of culture and methodological priorities focused on close examination of the artifact, which have been carried over from several of these founding fields into vernacular architecture studies, potentially limit our ability to address questions of gender and difference.

Unified Culture

Scholars of vernacular architecture, as well as those in the associated fields of cultural landscapes and material culture, work from the axiom that we can learn about a culture by examining the things made and used by members of the culture. Culture includes all aspects of the way of life of a given community, including beliefs, social structures, and practices. As material culture and vernacular architecture scholar Henry Glassie argues, things, including the built environment, are "culture made material"; therefore, by studying objects, buildings, and landscapes, we can learn about a culture's beliefs and actions.[6] By studying artifacts rather than words, we get a fuller picture of a culture. Artifacts reflect the lives of the illiterate as well as those whose words have not been saved. They also embody aspects of culture that are not written down, including beliefs that are taken for granted by members of a culture and aspects of culture that may be embarrassing or taboo.[7] Gender is a central organizing element of culture, so this principal of seeing culture through artifacts is also central to exploring gender in vernacular architecture.

However, assumptions about how culture functions can limit the ability to see the lives of the less powerful, including women and gender nonconformists. Vernacular architecture studies tends to use a model of culture with roots in folklore and anthropology, fields which examine clearly defined societies and conventionally focus on societies that are insular or isolated. In this model, whether culture is defined as "ideas, values, and beliefs" or as "ways of doing things," it is understood to be shared by all members of a society.[8] A limitation of this view is that it flattens out both power differentials and the distinctions among subgroups within a culture, potentially missing differences in ideas, values, and beliefs within a culture. As I discuss in more detail below, insofar as vernacular architecture studies focuses on a building's materiality and structure, it privileges the ideas, values, and beliefs of those with the resources to shape the more permanent elements of the built environment.

The geographer and cultural landscape scholar Pierce Lewis argues that culture is a "whole — a unity — like an iceberg with many tips protruding above the surface of the water," and therefore almost any item in the human landscape can be studied to learn about that culture.[9] However, each item will tell only partial stories, and it is easy for these stories to be dominated by the more powerful people within a society unless we pay close attention. Feminist anthropologists have shown that classic studies which purported to describe a culture fully were incomplete and misleading because they were based on the words and actions of men alone. For example, Annette Weiner revisited Bronislaw Malinowski's classic study of exchange in the culture of the Trobriand Islands of Papua New Guinea. She found that he and other male anthropologists had entirely missed the significance of women's wealth, thus misinterpreting the dynamics of exchange within Trobriand culture.[10] When we study the built environment, we need to make sure not to duplicate this kind of partial vision.

This issue is often addressed in American studies and cultural studies by focusing on a particular subculture or on a particular group within a culture, such as women or children. However, this approach still leaves the dominant understanding of culture untouched, in essence defining a culture as the ideas, values, and beliefs of the more powerful and relegating the ideas, values, and beliefs of the less powerful to subcultural status. When starting from the built environment, difference within a culture is often addressed by finding buildings that are connected to a particular subculture. Black experiences, for example, are studied by examining the buildings in all-Black freedom towns, while gender is examined by exploring an all-male space such as a dormitory for railroad workers.[11] While this kind of focus (discussed in chapter 3) allows the scholar to hone in on race or gender, it still makes for a very partial view, as most raced and gendered experiences are not in buildings used only by one race or gender, and most segregated spaces are not created and controlled by those who live within them. Thinking beyond segregated spaces requires more complex ways of thinking about culture, and especially about power differentials within a culture.

Fieldwork

Of the founding fields of vernacular architecture studies, art history, preservation, and material culture studies have traditionally been rooted in connoisseurship, a deep knowledge about the origins, date, and cultural context of artworks or material objects that is based on close attention to details of form, technique, and material. When exploring ordinary buildings, connoisseurship is based on fieldwork and is demonstrated through close knowledge of building techniques including brickwork, framing, and cladding. Thus, a core method for vernacular architecture studies has been building-based fieldwork, in which a building is minutely explored and recorded through measured drawings and photography, with close attention paid to details of materials and construction methods (figure 1.1). Indeed, in their 2005 *Invitation to Vernacular Architecture,* Thomas Carter and Elizabeth Collins Cromley present this sort of fieldwork as the essence of vernacular architecture studies and devote nearly half the book to detailed instruction in building-based fieldwork.

The centrality of this sort of fieldwork can be traced in part to the importance of historic preservation and folklore as major founding disciplines for vernacular architecture studies.[12] Building-oriented fieldwork is one of the core techniques of historic preservation, and attention

FIG. 1.1. Students in a University of Virginia fieldwork class measuring woodwork, 2016. Photograph by Andrew Johnston.

to details of material and technique are traditionally used by preservationists to date buildings and describe their histories. Careful measuring is also evident in folklore studies of the 1970s, including the seminal work of Henry Glassie on eighteenth-century Virginia houses and of John Michael Vlach on the shotgun house and its links to Haiti and Africa.[13] Both of these studies use careful measurements of buildings as a basis for determining cultural patterns, arguing that in the size and proportion of the walls of a house and a room we can see the methods and deep historical memory of their builders. In addition, both preservationists and folklorists employ attention to details of technique and materials to determine the ethnic origins of buildings. For example, the cultural geographer Fred Kniffen, one of the founding scholars of vernacular architecture studies, used differences in log cabin notching techniques to map the migration of different ethnic groups within the US.[14]

Methodologically, the primacy of building-based fieldwork as the necessary core of vernacular architecture studies threatens to marginalize other methods that can be more useful for getting at the experiences of women and other marginalized people. A close description of buildings through building-based fieldwork expands the information available about the built environment and gives important clues about how buildings are organized, built, and transformed over time. However, because it primarily records how things are built, it tends to privilege the actions and decisions of men, who do the majority of building. In addition, this materialist approach prioritizes the physical over the experiential and the performative, running the risk of making the people who first built a building always more important than those who have used it in the many years since it was built.[15] When looking at mass-culture buildings in particular, the decision-makers are more powerful people within their culture, who have money and authority and are more likely to be male and White. Privileging traditional fieldwork affects what and who we can see. For example, if we focus just on the buildings of Chicago's Little Village, currently a Mexican American neighborhood, we will mostly see the decision-making of the Eastern European immigrants who built them in the late nineteenth and early twentieth centuries. But if we examine instead how people live in them now, including ephemeral elements of the cityscape such as vendor carts, we will be able to see the contemporary Mexican American cultural landscape.[16]

It gets even more complicated when we want to focus on gender. Neighborhoods and communities are often organized by class, ethnicity, and race, and members of a household usually share these facets of identity. These identities are often organized spatially; therefore, the buildings within a particular neighborhood can speak to a shared identity, although imperfectly. However, communities organized by gender are extremely rare and specialized. Most people live in households and neighborhoods with others of a different gender. Gender is a cross-cutting category within social groups, rather than an isolatable community, and therefore using an approach that focuses on buildings that belong to a particular community is poorly suited to studying gender.

To study gender well, we should question the primacy that we have often given traditional fieldwork, expanding what kinds of research can be at the center of vernacular architecture studies. A wide range of research methods, including documentary research, oral histories, and analyses of visual evidence, have long been part of vernacular architecture, but they are too often framed primarily as ways to augment building-based fieldwork.[17] Case studies in this book show how putting other methods at the center can allow us to more fully consider gender and difference within the built environment. This book also suggests ways of reading all kinds of sources, including fieldwork, against the grain, looking at power relations and understanding the material record as not truth per se but the record of the more powerful. A wide range of methods are useful not only for researching gender, but also for approaching other axes of difference within our culture with more subtlety. If we were to focus only on mining camps, YMCAs, lesbian communes, and convents, we would clearly get a very incomplete picture of gender in the built environment. But only studying enclaves defined by race, ethnicity, or class also limits our understanding of the built environment of mixed communities and shared cultural landscapes. Thinking beyond traditional fieldwork will give us more tools with which to understand the lived experience of the ordinary built environment of the complex, global world in which we live.

Gender

To study gender in vernacular architecture, we first need to have a working definition of what we mean by gender. Currently, the term gender is often used as a euphemism for biological sex, but the word gender first began to be used by feminist scholars in the 1970s and 1980s precisely to distinguish between biological sex and the cultural attributes and social roles associated with having male or female bodies.[18] The distinction between sex and gender is important because it helps scholarship to move beyond essentialist ideas of femininity and masculinity based on biology. For example, many evolutionary biologists and some psychologists have argued that women are naturally more nurturing because they give birth to and breastfeed children. Similarly, the psychologist Erik Erikson contended that biology determined differences he saw in children's play, in which boys tended to build towers and girls enclosures.[19] Gender theorists would argue in contrast that it is the cultural norms of female nurturance and the different types of toys and play that have been offered to and praised in girls and boys that explains these observed differences. While scholars now understand that biological sex is more complex than a simple male/female divide, the distinction between the sexed body and the social roles that are imposed onto that sexed body remains useful.[20] In particular, by distinguishing between physical facts and cultural categories, using the term gender helps us to understand that gender structures are historically and culturally contingent, and thus mutable.

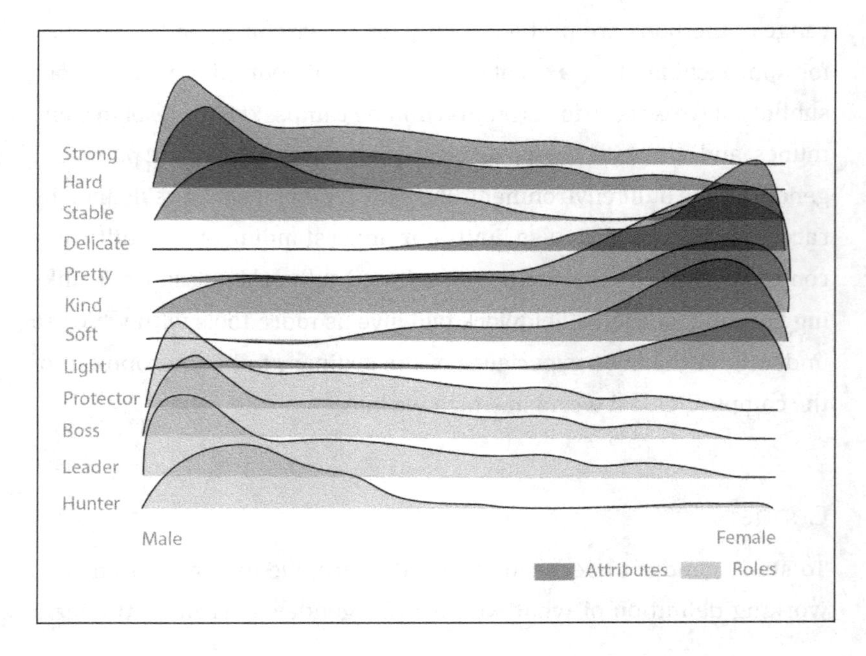

FIG. 1.2. Gender structures, which define the cultural meanings of gender, are based on a wide range of attributes, roles, and behaviors, each of which is associated to varying degrees with masculinity or femininity. Conceptual drawing by Tabi Summers.

By gender structures, I mean the underlying logic and social mechanisms of what it means to be male or female, masculine or feminine, within a particular culture. Attributes, roles, and ways of behaving are all tied up together within gender structures (figure 1.2). For example, the qualities of softness, lightness, warmth/caring, and servility are all gendered female in current American culture. They can be expressed bodily through long hair; flowing dresses; graceful movements; soft, lilting speech; and markers of physical containment such as crossed ankles. They can also translate into gendered roles, such as mother, nurse, waitress, secretary, and elementary school teacher. They are embodied in norms, such as the expectations for women to speak more indirectly, to be nurturing, and to put others ahead of themselves. Gender is a major dimension through which cultures are organized, and structures how people, activities, and even objects function and are understood. Gender structures are extremely powerful, but not monolithic, and they change over time.

Not only are gender structures culturally and historically specific, but they also overlap with other social categories within their time and culture. The idea of intersectionality, coined by Kimberlé Crenshaw and elaborated on by multiple scholars, notably Patricia Hill Collins, is useful for thinking about how gender intersects with other categories of power and difference, including race, class, and age. Intersectionality goes beyond an additive understanding of comparative privilege, in which Whiteness, masculinity, having an able body, etc. determine your place on a spectrum of privilege. Rather, as social categories of power intersect, they create unique and particular intersectional categories that may have more privilege in some situations and less in others (figure 1.3).[21]

While Crenshaw, a legal theorist, focuses on questions of privilege and oppression, the idea of intersectionality is also useful for discussing the specific attributes of cultural categories like gender when they intersect with other cultural categories. What it means to be female or male is not the same for all members of a culture. As Sojourner Truth invokes in her speech "Ain't I a Woman?," while White womanhood in the mid-nineteenth century was associated with helplessness and fragility, Black womanhood was associated with strength and a nearly infinite capability to labor.[22] The sexist virgin-whore dichotomy has been similarly racialized, with the purity of White womanhood constructed

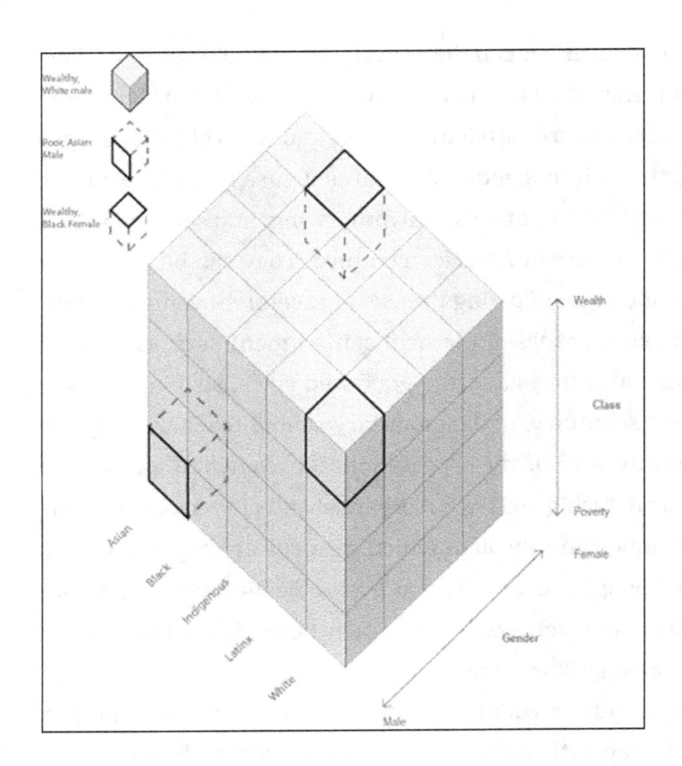

FIG. 1.3. Identities intersect; any one person is simultaneously part of several categories (many more than the three sketched here). Gender, race, class, ethnicity, ability, nationality, sexuality, and other social identities combine to create distinct experiences and cultural assumptions. Conceptual diagram of matrix of intersections of social categories by Tabi Summers.

in relationship to a sexualized image of Black women.[23] Similarly, both age and disability complicate understandings of gender; small children, postmenopausal women, and people living with disabilities are often treated as ungendered or desexed.[24] The social category of gender is not uniform, it is lumpy — it takes on different attributes depending on the other characteristics of an individual and depending on the positionality of the one ascribing the attributes. Gender, therefore, is not a category that we can isolate on its own; we always need to pay attention to the particularities of class, race, sexuality, age, ability, and other aspects of difference to understand the details of a specific historical gendered category or experience.

In contemporary discourse, there are two major interlocking ways of understanding gender: as an identity and as a social structure. These two approaches overlap in that they both address gender as a set of social norms and roles, but they differ in focus. Gender understood as an identity focuses on how an individual experiences themself as a gendered being. At the core of this experience is a personal sense of identity, but this approach also engages with how that personal sense interacts with how genders are socially assigned and understood and the cultural norms and social roles attached to gender.[25] The identity-focused approach works towards a personal and cultural liberation from tightly constrained ideas of gender. It borrows from Judith Butler's theory of performativity, which argues that gender is created through collective and repeated acts; that gender is not something that is, but rather something that is done.[26] This unties gender and biological sex and provides a glimpse of the possibility of doing gender other ways. However, Butler's vision is not of a free play of gender performance. Rather, Butler emphasizes that doing gender "wrong" is punished, because gender performance always happens in the context of gender ideology.

An approach that focuses instead on gender structures examines gender ideology, asking how gender norms and roles function socially and how they interact with other structures of difference and inequality. A structural approach is focused on systems of power and oppression and broad, collective social structures more than on how they are experienced by an individual. Feminists working with a structural approach also hope for liberation, but they believe that we need to understand how gendered power structures work in order to undo them and imagine ways beyond them. As structures of power, gender structures often work in concert with other power structures to cause, reproduce, and mask oppression; working intersectionally requires recognizing that gender is not just a category, but also part of larger structures of power and oppression. Both approaches most usefully understand gender identities and gender structures not in isolation, but rather as they intersect with other social identities and structures. These two broad approaches to exploring gender are also interdependent. Gender can only be experienced as an identity within the context of social structures that give gender meaning. Social structures gain much of their significance in how they are experienced by individuals within a culture.

Exploring gender in the built environment most often begins with questions of broader gender structures, of how gender norms and roles are reflected in and enforced by the material environment.[27] However, the built environment also shapes the experience of individuals and thereby helps to shape gendered identities. Our experience of space is not neutral; as Iris Marion Young has argued, how we learn to hold our body in space (something we learn in part from the built and designed environment) has consequences to our sense of self and our power in the world.[28] In addition, by making abstract gender ideologies material, the built environment helps them to appear natural and commonsense. As will be explored in more detail in this book, we learn gender in part from the built environment, which shapes our bodies, our understanding of the world, and our sense of our own place within it.

Exploring Gender in Vernacular Architecture

Every aspect of a building or cultural landscape and its life course is potentially affected by gender and can be approached through a gendered lens. In this book, I will take you through multiple approaches to examining gender in vernacular architecture, exploring what models of gender each approach engages with, explaining the insights scholars have made using these approaches, postulating on what each approach promises for future research, and introducing useful methods for studying gender in the built environment. This book will help you understand multiple ways to use a gendered lens to enrich your understanding of the built environment and how it is entangled with cultural structures of power and difference.

Chapter 2, "Gender and the Shaping of Space," explores research that focuses on the importance of the gender of the creators, clients, and shapers of vernacular architecture, including female architects. This approach is based on understanding gender as an identity and examining how this identity helps to shape the built environment. It helps us to understand how both men and women have helped to create the gendered built environment and challenges us to question our assumptions about who creates the built environment and how.

Chapter 3, "Single-Gender Spaces," shifts to a model of gender as ideology. Similar to work on spaces segregated by race, class, or ethnicity, studies of single-gender spaces allow us to focus in on gender and to pay attention to spaces controlled by the less powerful. These single-gender realms are relatively atypical but can provide insight into the relationship between gender ideology, or dominant cultural understandings of gender, and built form.

Chapter 4, "Mixed-Gender Spaces," continues the exploration of how vernacular architecture both reflects and enforces heterosexual gendered ideologies, focusing on mixed-gender spaces. It demonstrates how sources that illuminate how gender was understood and practiced in a particular time and place can be combined with a close reading of buildings to illuminate how gender ideology has been made physical in vernacular architecture.

Chapter 5, "Queer Spaces," goes beyond heteronormative readings of the built environment. It investigates how to read vernacular architecture against the heterosexual grain, exploring some of the ways queer spaces, including apartments, bedrooms, bookstores, and bars, have been fashioned through both use and design. It challenges us to explore spaces as layered with meanings and to understand that often use, even ephemeral use, can be more important than the materiality of a building in exploring the cultural meanings of vernacular architecture.

Chapter 6, "Researching Gendered Experience," focuses not on a particular kind of space, but rather on ways of approaching analyzing any space, including those discussed in earlier chapters. Spaces are experienced differently by people with different identities. Experience is how the built environment shapes culture; it is through the use of spaces that embody gender ideologies that these ideologies become naturalized. This chapter explores the sources, from traces of use and physical form through diaries, memoirs, and oral histories, that researchers can use to understand the ephemeral world of gendered experiences.

2

GENDER AND THE SHAPING OF SPACE

In the design professions, a primary approach to thinking about gender and the built environment has been to focus on the gender of the designer. The overwhelming masculinity and Whiteness of the design profession, combined with popular ideas about men's supposedly natural spatial and technical ability, can make it difficult to imagine architecture as a female and multiracial profession. In this context, feminists have worked to recover the suppressed history of woman architects, a central task in the larger project of rewriting the canon.[1] In addition to recovering historical architects such as Julia Morgan (1872–1957) and Eileen Gray (1878–1976), profiles of contemporary women designers have helped to refute the equation of architect and maleness, as well as to interrogate the barriers women and non-Whites face within the design professions.[2]

In explorations of the gender of shapers of the built environment one question is "What difference does it make whether these shapers are female or male?" This approach is based on understanding gender as an identity and examining how this identity helps to shape the built environment. While a few writers have argued for an essential difference based on the body (often building off the ideas of French philosopher Luce Irigaray), more often this approach is grounded in the different enculturation of women and men.[3] For example, building on the work of feminist social scientists, Karen Franck argues that in designs by women we can trace an understanding of the world through connectedness rather than division, as well as a valuing of complexity, flexibility, and care.[4] These attributes can be traced in part to women's socialization as caregivers and the complexity of the labor of running a household (often while also working outside it).

While much of the research and writing on gender and design has focused on women's participation in formal professions, a recognition of the barriers to women's ability to join the formal design professions has meant that this work has expanded to encompass ways women have shaped space beyond the formal role of architect, landscape architect, interior designer, or planner. These studies have looked at women activists, reformers, journalists, and clients to explore how they have shaped architecture and the built environment. Exploration of the role of women as clients in particular has served to interrupt the narrative of architecture as the expression of a singular (male) architect/artist by examining the ways that the built environment often reflects the desires and ideas of the client as much or more than the ideas of the architect. For example, Alice Friedman grounds her reading of the iconic 1924 Rietveld-Schroeder house in Utrecht in an exploration of Truus Schroeder's radical ideas about childrearing and family, expressed in spaces like the remarkably flexible upstairs, where bedrooms and kitchen flow into one with the folding of walls. She argues that we cannot interpret this house merely as the expression of Rietveld's de Stijl aesthetic, but rather as a collaboration between Rietveld as architect and Schroeder as client.[5]

Exploring the role of gender in the shaping of the built environment beyond the formal design professions means often blurring the line between formal, high-style architecture and vernacular architecture, as reformers' and journalists' work has often affected the ordinary built environment as much or more than high-style architecture. For example, the writer, reformer, and planning professor Catherine Bauer Wurster's 1934 book *Modern Housing* can be understood both as a manifesto for architectural modernism and as an influential argument for the provision of public housing, which helped to shape the future of mass housing in the US. Similarly, as editor of *House Beautiful*, Ethel Power both promoted the popularity of architectural modernism and helped shape the built environment of ordinary housing and the role of women in influencing the built environment.[6]

Because research that starts from the gender of makers is part of a larger project to expand beyond the man-made environment, most scholars working from this approach focus primarily on the role of women in shaping the built environment. Using this approach to explore vernacular architecture helps us to overcome sexist assumptions about who makes decisions about the vernacular built environment and who does the work of building. Using a range of sources beyond the built environment itself, we can explore how the everyday built environment has been shaped by women as well as by men, getting a more accurate understanding of whose culture is being reflected by buildings.

Women Building

The profession of building is male dominated, and we tend to assume that building work is something done by men. However, depending on cultural context and how we define building, this is not always the case. Many vernacular building traditions use accessible techniques, and the process of building is often collective, with each member of a community participating according to their skill level. Rina Swentzell writes of the construction of houses at her home village, Santa Clara Pueblo, "everyone participated, without exception — men, women, children, and elders. Anybody could build a house or any necessary structure."[7] Similarly, memoirs of settlement on the American frontier in the late nineteenth century describe immigrant men and women working together on the building of their sod houses (figure 2.1).[8]

In Africa, designing and building housing is often traditionally women's domain. In her study of African nomadic architecture, architect and historian Labelle Prussin traces the role of women in creating, erecting, and furnishing nomadic tent houses in multiple nomadic tribes. The strength of the relationship between a woman and a house is such that in the Rendille tribe, a man cannot have a house without a wife, and the verb "to marry" is synonymous with the verb "to build."[9] Similarly, Himba women in Namibia and Ndebele women in South Africa create, furnish, and decorate houses, and the houses are considered to be their domain, as are the nomadic houses Prussin explores.[10] Prussin argues that with sedentation, women in these tribes often lose power as their role as creators and shapers of space is weakened. As with many studies of vernacular architecture outside the West, Prussin's study is based on ethnographic fieldwork, in which anthropologists live with the people they are studying and combine observation, interviews, study of objects, and their own experience to try to fully describe a culture.[11]

FIG. 2.1. A sod house, like this one in Nebraska, is made by cutting pieces of sod from the prairie and piling it up to make walls. Sod houses were generally built by the people who used them, rather than by any sort of expert. This sod house was the home of homesteader Lizzie Chrisman, second from left. The Chrisman sisters, 1886, photograph by Solomon Butcher. Courtesy of Nebraska State Historical Society Photograph Collection.

Even in the context of male-dominated building trades, we can see the influence of a broader range of builders if we expand our understanding of building beyond the creation of structure. Finishes and furnishings, including paint, curtains, floor coverings, screens, furniture, and decoration, are all part of the creation of space, as is the shaping of the landscape of which a building is part. The meaning and use of space is only hinted at by the names on a plan or the relationships among rooms; it is how the rooms are finished, furnished, and used that gives them meaning. Textiles, decorating, and gardening are all aspects of the creation of vernacular architecture that have often been dominated by women. If we expand our understanding of what vernacular architecture is to incorporate interiors and gardens, culturally evocative aspects of the built environment that, although often more fugitive, are essential to understanding how people dwell in place, we will more fully recognize the role of women in constructing vernacular architecture.

FIG. 2.2. Claim shacks were simple, rough, typically one-room buildings, fulfilling the minimum needs of a homesteader while meeting the legal requirements of the Homestead Act. Woman at claim shack. Courtesy of South Dakota State Historical Society, South Dakota Digital Archives (2010-12-09-017).

Women Shaping Everyday Space

Exploring the role of women as builders and designers of vernacular architecture requires both challenging our gendered assumptions about the built environment and using methods and sources that have not always been part of vernacular architecture research. Rebecca Sample Bernstein and Carolyn Torma's investigation of the role of women in the creation of farm buildings in South Dakota found many ways that conventional understandings of how these places were created were lacking.[12] Bernstein and Torma found evidence that women were often the prime decision-makers as to the form of farmhouses and buildings, contrary to the assumptions of most scholars. Remarkably, 12%–30% of homestead claims in the prairies and plains were made by single women, which challenges the usual image of the West as settled by men and nuclear families.

In addition to these women's farmsteads, buildings in family farms were also strongly influenced by women, whether as builders or as

FIG. 2.3. Harriet Ward house, Custer County. In comparison to the shack her husband originally built, this house is substantial and multiroomed, allowing for more polite ways of living. Courtesy of South Dakota State Historical Society, South Dakota Digital Archives (2014-05-09-319).

decision-makers. European immigrants who settled in the Plains more often came from rural contexts than Americans moving west, which meant that they had more knowledge and skill in vernacular building. Biographies of immigrant female settlers in the Dakotas include many descriptions of cooperative building, in which women were as involved in the process of building sod and adobe buildings as men were. American migrant women were somewhat less likely to be involved in the building process but still had a strong influence on building form. In oral histories, many married women complained of their husbands' poor designs for houses and demanded changes or entirely new houses that were more functional and better fit their social standing. For example, when Anna Langhorne Waltz joined her husband in Burke, South Dakota, in 1911, she found that the two-room frame house he had built was poorly set up for cooking, so she refused to cook until he had improved it. When Mrs. Harriet Ward travelled to Custer, South Dakota, to join her new husband, she refused to stay unless he replaced his small shack with a modern two-story home more befitting her status as an educated American woman (figures 2.2, 2.3).

Because men usually do the majority of building work in the US, it is often assumed that they also determine its form; therefore, ethnic houses and barns are often seen as evidence of the ethnicity of the male head of household. However, several of the traditional Danish *parstuga* houses and associated large horse and dairy barns in North Dakota were built by non-Danish men. Bernstein and Torma found that in fact *parstuga* houses were associated with Danish women more than with Danish men, which suggests that even when men did the physical work of building a house, women often determined its form. This association was confirmed by oral histories, including an interview with a Danish woman who insisted that her Norwegian husband build a Danish *parstuga* for their family. Through their oral history interviews, Bernstein and Torma found further evidence to argue that in these Scandinavian immigrant communities, women were the bearers of ethnic architectural tradition and shaped the vernacular built environment to match their traditions. For example, a Finnish woman, Eva Larson, described telling her Norwegian husband and his brother how to build a sauna on their property in the 1930s. Similarly, a study of the transformation of village housing in Indonesia for tourism purposes found that women were often the prime decision-makers there, in large part because they were understood as being the keepers of cultural values that need to be preserved.[13] These studies suggest that we should be careful not to assume that the people doing the work of building a vernacular building are the decision-makers as to its form. Evidence suggests that these decisions are often shared and sometimes made by women; we will not know who made the decisions about a particular building without research, and it is therefore best to begin with an assumption of shared decision-making.

Gender-Based Organizations

While it has been common for men to act as clients for builders, whether as individuals, as business owners, or as leaders of institutions, it has historically been rarer for women, particularly beyond the female-associated realm of the household. When women have determined the form of the nondomestic built environment, it has often been as members of women's organizations, including clubs and philanthropic organizations. Like their male counterparts, such as the Masons, the Lions, and the YMCA, women's organizations have built edifices both to present themselves publicly to the world and to provide a dedicated space for their activities.

The Mormon Relief Society is an excellent example of a women's organization functioning as a client. Between 1861 and 1921, Relief Society women built over 120 Society halls as well as a wide range of buildings to support the public, including hospitals, libraries, granaries, and almshouses. In her study of the 1868 Fifteenth Ward Society Hall, Carolyn Butler-Palmer argues that through their building, Mormon women shaped the public life of Salt Lake City, made a space for their own political speech and debate, and made a claim for themselves as

FIG. 2.4. The Fifteenth Ward Relief Society Hall, in Salt Lake City, Utah, is a resolutely commercial building, from the prominent lettering on its façade to the glass-fronted store on its first floor. The goods displayed outside the shop as well as in the windows further emphasize that this is a store above all. Used by permission, Utah State Historical Society.

FIG. 2.5. Postcard view of Main Street, Marlette, Michigan, early 1900s. The shops lining this street, like the Fifteenth Ward Society Hall, are two stories, with a glass-fronted shop below and a hall or offices above. The prominent corniced façades echo that on the Society Hall as well.

members of the public and as businesswomen.[14] This claim was countered by the Mormon church's decree in 1921 that each Relief Society should meet within the local ward meetinghouse, a space controlled by men, rather than in their own Society hall.

To understand the significance of the Relief Society Hall, Butler-Palmer reads its architecture in the context of the minutes and ledgers of the Relief Society. These papers reflect the desires, identity, and cultural agenda of the women themselves, in their own words. They express the concerns of their work with the Society and their priorities in the creation of the hall. The siting of the hall at the center of the ward; their desire that the hall contain both a meeting hall above and a store below; and their professionalism in dealing with buying land, soliciting a design, and contracting with a builder are all notable in their papers. The centrality of the site reflects their vision of themselves as central to the community, while their professionalism and combination of shop and hall reflect their identity as businesswomen and members of the public in their own right.

The architecture of the Fifteenth Ward Relief Society Hall in Salt Lake City reflects the Relief Society women's self-presentation as businesswomen (figure 2.4). It is a two-story building with a meeting hall

FIG. 2.6. While the small-town Manti South Relief Society Ladies' House is just one story, its false front, large windows, and prominent lettering demonstrate its ties to commercial, not residential, architecture. Photograph c. 1920, Church of Jesus Christ of Latter-Day Saints Church History Catalogue.

above and a shop below, very much in line with typical commercial buildings of the era, in which a shop with large windows and a center entrance is topped with a space that could provide offices or a rental hall (figure 2.5). The prominent lettering on the cornice announces that the building is created by and houses the Relief Society, proclaiming the Society women's importance in the public space of the street. Other Relief Society halls similarly made use of this commercial architectural form, with a meeting space above and a store below. Even small halls in rural areas had a resolutely commercial form, expressing the public and businesslike status of the women of the Relief Society (figure 2.6). The meeting hall was used by the women of the Society not only for religious and charitable purposes, but also as a space to make goods they could sell and as a permanent office from which to run their businesses, which could include managing grocery stores, cultivating silk, farming, and functioning as landlords.[15] Their status as businesswomen helped to support their legitimacy as members of the public, and their meeting space meant that they had a location for debate among themselves about important political matters, including women's suffrage and national anti-polygamy legislation. The hall played an important role in women's lives, which we can better understand by examining its architecture as an expression of the desires of its female clients. Making use of historical archives, particularly the records of the Relief Society, gives access to those desires that are not directly observable in the buildings themselves and helps to give a context for reading their architecture. Reading the buildings from the point of view of the clients, not the builders, allows us to see how these buildings functioned both as statements about women's abilities and sense of self and as spaces that made women's public activities possible.

Institution Builders

Many women's organizations, as well as some individual founders, presented themselves publicly through institutional buildings that they shaped, much as the Relief Society presented themselves through their halls. An example of women as clients for major institutional buildings is presented by the Grey Nuns (Soeurs Grises), a Canadian religious order. Their enormous and imposing Mother House, in Montreal, was built between 1868 and 1901 (figure 2.7). The Mother House housed a convent, a hospital, an orphanage, elderly housing, and other services for the indigent, as well as a chapel and multiple ancillary services such as a laundry, a bakery, a printing and bookbinding shop, and farm buildings. It was built on a prominent site in a prosperous neighborhood and was significantly larger than any other Montreal institution. Its symmetrical grey stone façade, centered on a Palladian-towered chapel, demands respect as a public building and expresses the power and importance of the Grey Nuns. Tania Martin's research on this building and other buildings built by this order is grounded in the archives of the Grey Nuns, where letters, reports, annals, and plans provide insight into the building and decision-making process. Using these archives, she found that the Grey Nuns took a very active role in determining the building's form, even supervising construction sites. Because they were projecting

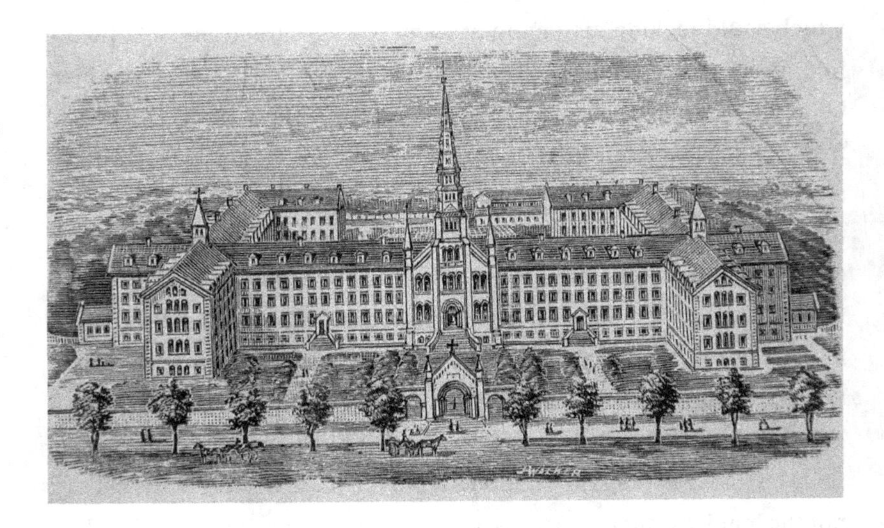

FIG. 2.7. The Mother House of the Grey Nuns in Montreal is a massive institutional building that demonstrated the importance of the order and its extensive charitable work. Print by John Henry Walker, c. 1885. McCord Stewart Museum, M930.50.5.559.

the humility of their calling and their collective anonymity (as well as their significant social power) through their Mother House, the Grey Nuns pushed back against the architect's initial designs, choosing a larger, plainer building that prioritized service over show.[16]

YWCA buildings similarly present women's organizations to the public as solid and sober institutions. Studying historic postcards of YWCAs provides insight into how these women-run organizations presented themselves. The majority present their balanced, symmetrical buildings as a symbol of the organization (figure 2.8). Their style matches many other institutional buildings within their cities, typically three-to-six-story brick or stone buildings with a single substantial entrance and a tall ground floor. YWCAs gained this presence in the early twentieth century, previously having been often housed within reused grand domestic edifices (figure 2.9). This transformation from a domestic to an institutional image, expressed through buildings, happens simultaneously with women's increasing participation in both higher education and the workforce, and with women's gradual gaining of the right to vote in the US. Significantly, while the first Black YWCA branch, in Dayton, Ohio, was housed in a large house, by 1920 the Phyllis Wheatley YWCA in Washington, DC, the first and only independent Black YWCA in the US, was housed in a substantial brick purpose-built edifice that communicated the stature of Black women and the Black community (figure 2.10).

Both the Grey Nuns and YWCA members created institutional buildings not only as a symbol of themselves, but also to house their activi-

FIG. 2.8. The Dayton, Ohio, YWCA is a picture of middle-class respectability and prosperous permanence. It is significantly larger and more modern than the buildings surrounding it and could easily be mistaken for a hotel. It presents the YWCA as a solid, respectable, and modern organization. Postcard of Dayton, OH, YWCA, c. 1910.

FIG. 2.9. Many YWCAs, like this one in Binghamton, New York, were initially housed in repurposed grand domestic buildings. Postcard of Binghamton, NY, YWCA, c. 1908.

ties. These activities, including caring for the poor, healing the sick, and educating the young, are associated with culturally feminine roles of nurturance and motherhood, but within women-run institutions, these caring activities were professionalized and expanded outward from the family to the entire community. Female-run philanthropic institutions, including YWCAs and settlement houses, were usually led by the more powerful members of the community, who were well-to-do, nonimmigrant, and typically White. As philanthropists, they desired to serve and often reform others less powerful than themselves. When exploring the buildings created by these women-run institutions, it is

FIG. 2.10. The Phyllis Wheatley YWCA, in Washington, DC, was the first independent Black YWCA in the US. Its substantial but modestly decorated brick building communicates that this YWCA is here to stay. APK, CC BY-SA 3.0, https://creativecommons.org/licenses/by-sa/3.0, Wikimedia Commons.

important to be conscious of how questions of class, culture, and power intersect with gender within them, and to be aware of how the same spaces were often differently understood and experienced by those using them and those creating them.

The interior of the Mother House of the Gray Nuns was scientific in its sorting of people and in its use of modern technologies, expressing a dedication to order and professional efficiency. Residents of the building were sorted spatially by rank, role, gender, and age. The middle-class choir nuns were spatially distinguished from the working-class auxiliary nuns, and within each group, the ranks of postulant, novice, and professed slept in different spaces, with more of a separation from public space as nuns ascended through the ranks. Each of the populations served by the Grey Nuns (orphans, aged, destitute) was housed in a distinct wing, in spaces ordered by gender and, in the case of orphans, by age. This sorting out of populations allowed for a wide variety of ac-

Y. W. C. A. Residence Parlors, 30 Howard Street, Springfield, Mass.

FIG. 2.11. Even as they created spaces for independent women and opportunities for women to better themselves, YWCAs emphasized the importance of domesticity through interior decoration, as in the residence parlors of the Springfield, Massachusetts, YWCA. Postcard c. 1915.

tivities and people to be highly organized and tightly defined, reflecting both the highly ordered monastic life and the ideals of professionalism. The modernity and self-sufficiency of the Grey Nuns was visible in the range of activities they pursued and the steam- and gas-powered mechanisms they used, including steam-powered sewing and knitting machines and a steam-powered elevator. In addition to spaces such as a large steam laundry and kitchens that housed all the services needed to support its population, the Mother House also contained a range of other workshops, including a printing and bookbinding shop and a factory making candles, wax figurines, and religious relics. In these spaces, nuns ran large mechanical equipment and supervised workers, using their status as nuns to take on roles not ordinarily open to women.[17]

Purpose-built YWCAs usually served two populations: women who came to the Y for classes, physical recreation, club meetings, and sociability, and single women who resided there. In several cities, including New York and Los Angeles, separate auxiliary buildings were created just to house young working women. Building from scratch allowed YWCAs to better provide these services by including swimming pools and gymnasiums for physical recreation and by providing floors of secure purpose-built dwelling rooms with adequate privacy and plumbing. Even as YWCAs helped women to enter the workforce through housing

FIG. 2.12. (*facing page*) By 1906 the Hull House settlement in Chicago encompassed a wide range of activities in its complex, including club rooms, school rooms, a commercial kitchen, varied residences, an auditorium, and multiple workshops. It is nearly impossible to find the traces of the historic house at the core of this institutional complex. Plan from *Hull House Yearbook*, 1906–1907, 4.

and training and encouraged their physical strength, they also used domestic imagery to create a comfortable environment and to demonstrate middle-class ideals of femininity to their mixed-class users (figure 2.11).

While the Mother House of the Grey Nuns and twentieth-century YWCAs were built from scratch, many women's organizations have instead reworked existing buildings, whether through furnishing and use or by physically transforming them. An example of large-scale transformation is Hull House in Chicago, a settlement house founded in 1889 by Jane Addams and Ellen Gates Starr. While the settlement began with the grand house after which it is named, Addams and Starr had it enlarged continuously for many years, until the settlement took up a whole block and submerged the original building in a "rabbit warren" of brick institutional buildings that held an auditorium, a gymnasium, classrooms, a dining hall, workshops, housing for settlement workers and working mothers, boys' and girls' clubhouses, and a creche and kindergarten (figure 2.12). When the University of Illinois at Chicago campus was built in the 1960s, this complex was demolished and the original house at its core was restored to its pre–Hull House form and became a museum dedicated to Addams. The Hull House settlement work continued, but the spaces that had been core to its work became frozen in time as a museum. In creating the museum, the University erased Addams's architectural and social imprint and recast her far-reaching community-building work, expressed in large-scale brick buildings, as a form of Victorian domestic hospitality.[18]

Because many women-run charities focused on the family and the care of children, repurposing a domestic building was not only often a financially expedient choice, but also a symbolic one, making evident in architectural form that the charity work these organizations did was a natural and respectable extension of their organizers' status as mothers and as women. For example, the Ladies' Relief Society of Oakland turned a large middle-class farmhouse into an orphanage in the 1870s, raising it one floor to add a lower-level kitchen and dining room and renovating the other floors to provide a schoolroom and separate dormitory facilities for girls and boys. Even as they transformed the use and spatial arrangement of the building, they kept its domestic appearance, emphasizing its status as a children's home rather than as an institution.[19]

The impulse to reuse domestic buildings for new, more public purposes has continued well past the turn of the century. Many feminist

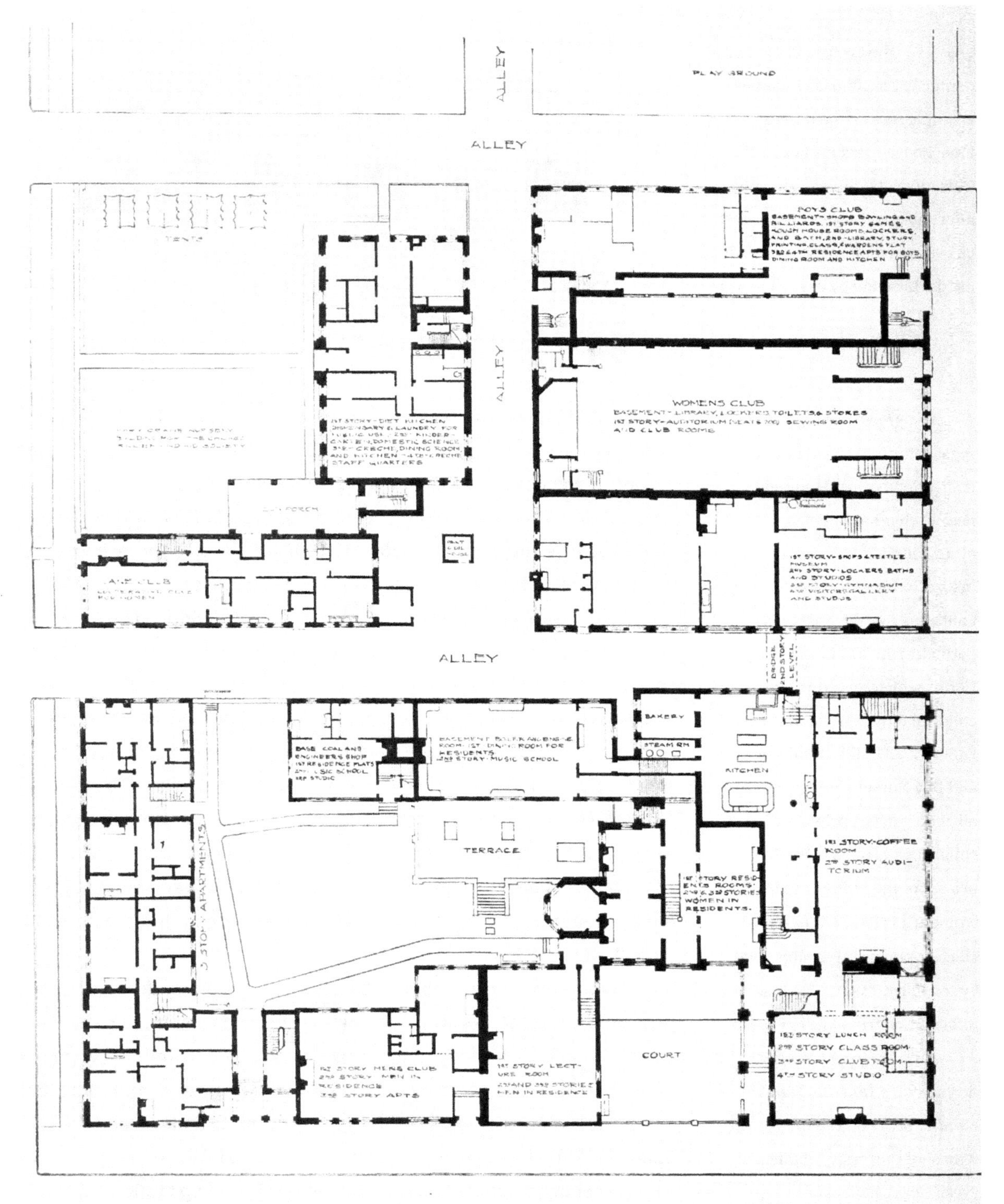

SCALE OF FEET

BLOCK PLAN OF HULL HOUSE

FIG. 2.13. The Crenshaw Women's Center in Los Angeles occupied a simple residential duplex that later housed various businesses. This modest building was both affordable and accessible, as well as easy to adapt to meet changing needs. Drawing by Jessica Sewell.

FIG. 2.14. (*facing page*) In the 1920s, multiple Black-run institutions were clustered near each other and near other religious and charitable institutions in West Oakland, California. On this map, 1 is the Catholic-run St. Vincent's Day Home, which served White children only; 2 is the Black-run Fannie Wall Children's Home and Day Nursery, which served all children, but primarily Black children; 3 is the Linden Street branch of the YWCA, run by Black women; 4 is Beth Eden Baptist church; and 5 marks sites used by the Black YMCA. Map based on information from Marta Gutman, *A City for Children: Women, Architecture, and the Charitable Landscapes of Oakland, 1850–1950* (Chicago: University of Chicago Press, 2014), figure 9.11.

women's centers that opened in the US in the 1970s also made use of repurposed domestic buildings. Arising out of consciousness-raising groups, which usually met in a member's home, these women's centers moved into domestic buildings within the neighborhoods they served, both because they were affordable but also to be as approachable and everyday as possible. For example, the Crenshaw Women's Center occupied one side of a one-story duplex in a lower-middle-class, mixed-race residential neighborhood in Los Angeles (figure 2.13). The organizers of the Crenshaw Women's Center did not change the building's structure, but added signage, replaced the back parking lot with a playground, and shifted the use of the rooms to accommodate meetings, office equipment, a library, and medical counseling. To maintain a comfortable, homelike atmosphere, they decorated with donated domestic furniture including a couch, armchairs, and beanbag chairs.[20] Blurring the line between domestic space and public actions, the Crenshaw Women's Center embodied the feminist slogan that the personal is political.

Daphne Spain argues that by transforming ordinary domestic space into political spaces for women's empowerment, women's centers, feminist health clinics, and feminist bookstores helped to improve women's status in the public realm by creating a feminist cultural landscape that supported women's rights to the city. It is useful to look beyond the singular building to explore its broader cultural landscape. In the case of the Crenshaw Women's Center, it spawned "Self-Help Clinic One" (later renamed the Feminist Women's Health Center), which offered abortions and other women's health services in the other half of the duplex and expanded to a second location in a two-story house a few blocks away.

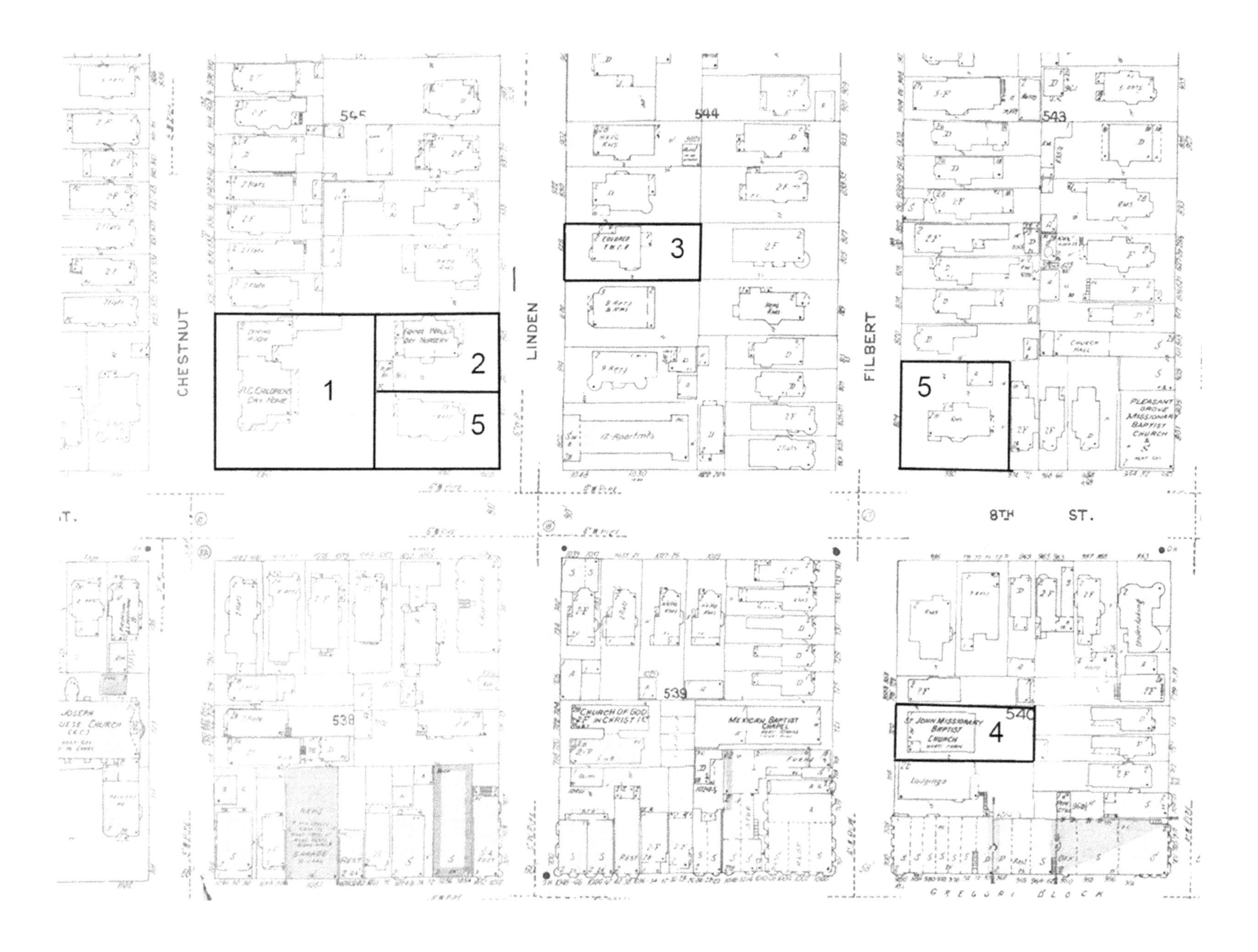

CHESTNUT
LINDEN
FILBERT
8TH ST.
1
2
3
4
5
5
538
539
540
543
544
545
R.C. CHILDREN'S DAY HOME
COLORED Y.W.C.A.
12 Apartments
CHURCH HALL
PLEASANT GROVE MISSIONARY BAPTIST CHURCH
CHURCH OF GOD IN CHRIST
MEXICAN BAPTIST CHAPEL
ST. JOHN MISSIONARY BAPTIST CHURCH
Lodgings
Undertaking
GREGORI BLOCK

In both locations, this clinic decorated using comfortable chairs, encouraging both waiting and recovering women to spend time in a waiting room furnished more like a living room.[21]

We can see a parallel landscape surrounding other buildings repurposed by women's groups earlier in the century. For example, in West Oakland, a wide range of cultural and service organizations clustered near the site of St. Vincent's Day Home, a Catholic day care run by the Sisters of the Holy Family (figure 2.14). St. Vincent's Day Home occupied a grand house and served White families of all ethnicities, providing care to up to 200 infants and children each day while their parents worked.[22] In 1928, the Fannie Wall Children's Home, run by the Northern Association of Colored Women's Clubs to serve both Black children and other children whose families were not comfortable with the Catholic church, relocated to an upper-middle-class house that shared a back fence with St. Vincent's. Across the street was the Linden branch of the YWCA, which served Black women; next door was one of two buildings occupied by the Black YMCA; and Beth Eden Baptist Church was a block away. Marta Gutman argues that we can understand this landscape of charity as evidence of how Black women made a place for themselves in public culture, demonstrating their ability to build institutions and simultaneously fighting segregation.[23]

Why Study the Gender of Shapers of the Built Environment?

The cultural landscapes anchored by women's institutions demonstrate one reason to pay attention to the identity of the shapers of the built environment. A building does not exist individually but is part of a larger cultural landscape, influencing the ways other buildings are used and understood as well as how the space between buildings is animated. In West Oakland, the Northern Association of Colored Women's Clubs' choice to locate the Fannie Wall Children's Home on Linden Street can be understood in multiple ways. In choosing a substantial domestic building to house the Children's Home, they were using a tactic used by many women's groups, associating their women-run institution with domesticity and class. This took on an extra valence because they were Black, so that through their respectability they were representing both their sex and their race. In choosing a site near other Black-run institutions, they were strengthening a Black civic sphere and a physical landscape of Black empowerment. In choosing a site that abutted a segregated, White-run institution, they were challenging St. Vincent's policies and prominence. We can only understand the significance of this building if we know that its use and physical reshaping was directed by Black middle-class women.

The examples discussed in this chapter also show the importance of treating the repurposing and reshaping of buildings as a moment of creation if we want to understand the role of women and the less powerful in the vernacular built environment. The building that housed the Fannie Wall Children's Home tells us more complex and important stories if we focus on its use as an orphanage and day care center rather than looking at it more narrowly as an example of a late Victorian upper-middle-class home.

Asking questions about who shaped the built environment allows us to get a more complex understanding of the ideology embodied within a given building. It is not enough to know that a building was created or shaped within a particular culture. Not everyone within a culture has the same beliefs; buildings participate in power struggles. For the Mormon women of the Relief Society, their buildings expressed their worth within their community and their ability to be part of the public realm. The fact that the church hierarchy decreed that they should not have buildings of their own illustrates the importance of these buildings as a statement. It is only by paying attention to the intent of the women who were patrons of the Relief Society buildings that we can understand why their similarity to ordinary downtown commercial buildings is so significant.

Information on shapers of space is not always easily accessible. As historians of women architects who collaborated with male architects have found, their contributions are often hidden in the discourse around their designs. But digging into primary records can often make women's roles, and those of other less powerful people, visible.[24] In addition, studies of women as clients, designers, and builders all suggest that we should avoid making assumptions about who decision-makers are. When the stories of the built environment are told largely by more prosperous White men, they are often incomplete, erasing the more diverse populations who are involved in its shaping.

3

SINGLE-GENDER SPACES

In order to study gender in vernacular architecture, many scholars have turned to single-gender spaces. Most of the built environment consists of spaces that are shared by men and women, even if unequally or in different roles. In these mixed spaces, it can be difficult for researchers to isolate gender as a variable. Single-gender spaces, in contrast, can be assumed to tell us something about the cultural meanings of the gender of the people by whom they are used. More than the spaces discussed in the last chapter, single-gender spaces tell us primarily about gender structures — about how masculinity and femininity, men and women, are understood within a culture — not about the gender identity of those using them. These gender structures are particularly visible when we can contrast similar spaces intended for men and for women, such as dormitories and public restrooms. Studying places such as women's colleges, women's waiting rooms, YMCAs, and men's clubs, then, can bring gender more clearly into focus than mixed-gender spaces. A single-gender space allows a focus on gender as a cultural category, much as studying a settlement or institution segregated by race, class, or ethnicity allows researchers to isolate Black, working-class, or immigrant cultures in contradistinction to the dominant (White, middle-class, Anglo-American) culture. In addition, given that most spaces have been shaped and controlled primarily by men, spaces such as women's clubs and convents that are shaped and controlled by women allow researchers to also explore the role of gender in the shaping of space, as we have seen in the previous chapter.

Single-gender spaces are most common when gender roles are in

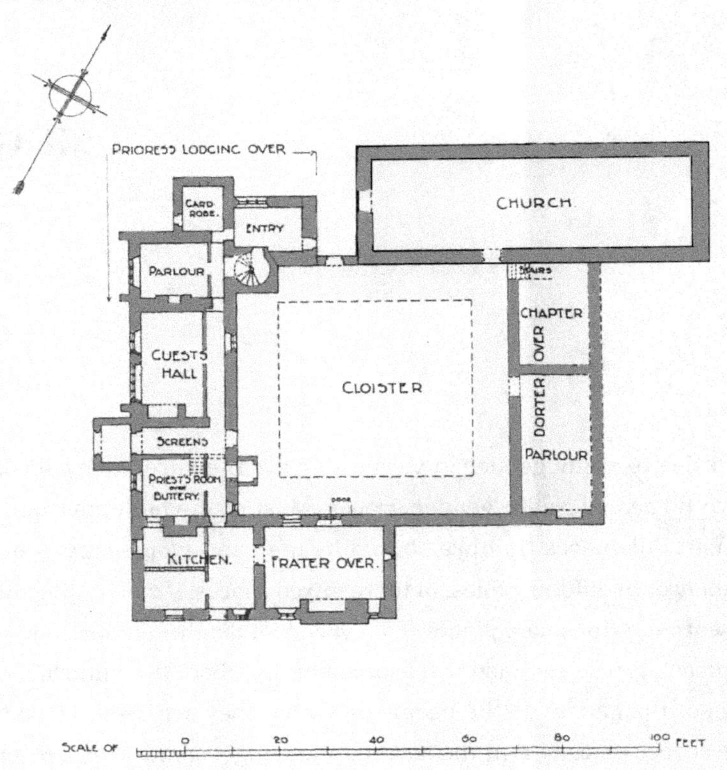

FIG. 3.1. The Plan of Kington St. Michael Priory, Wiltshire, UK, built between the twelfth and fifteenth centuries, is typical for a medieval English nunnery. The secluded chapter house and dormitory in the west range sits across the cloister from the more public-facing set of rooms in the east range, which include a space for a visiting priest, spaces for guests, and the prioress's rooms. The refectory and kitchen sit to the south, opposite a large church to the north. Like other monasteries, it is enclosed and cloistered, and its layout is quite like medieval monasteries for monks as well as those for nuns. Adapted from Harold Brakspear, "Excavations at Some Wiltshire Priories," *Archaeologica* 73, 1923. Public domain, Wikimedia Commons.

flux or when there is some other cultural need for gender differences to be clearly defined. Gendered space can help naturalize gender differences by making them concrete, just as pink and blue clothes and gendered toys help to naturalize gender differences between children. When people repeatedly find that spaces for men are in dark natural tones, with wood and leather dominant, while spaces for women are lighter, with more color, pattern, and adornment, this reinforces the idea that men and women are naturally different, with different tastes and desires. People are enculturated into gender roles in part through their experiences in single-gender spaces, with the organization and decoration of a space communicating to them about the nature of their particular gender role, reinforcing the activities and messages they experience within it. In addition to being gendered, this role, and the spaces that reflect it, are also classed, raced, marked by age, and historically and geographically specific.

FIG. 3.2. The west range of Kington St. Michael Priory resembles manor houses of the same period and is not immediately recognizable as a religious building. Drawing by Tabi Summers.

Studying Architecture to See Gender

The built environment embodies understandings of gender which can be excavated in order to more fully understand how gender is defined and lived in a particular cultural and historical context. For example, comparing men's and women's medieval British monastic buildings allows us to better understand the nature of gender and its intersections with social class in that period. Roberta Gilchrist argues that typically nunneries have been judged and studied using male monasteries as a standard; but if we instead focus on their particularities, we can understand nunneries in their own right and, in so doing, better understand the place of women religious within the church and broader society and how nuns may have understood themselves.[1]

Medieval English nunneries followed a standard model for monastic complexes, in which a cloister was surrounded by a church (usually to the south) and a series of ranges. Typically, the ranges included a chapter house to the east, a refectory opposite the church, and a west range that housed multiple uses, including a guest house and the prioress's rooms (figure 3.1). However, in many ways, nunneries followed manor house norms more than their male counterparts did. For example, they were often moated, and the architecture of the west range was usually modeled on secular manor houses (figure 3.2). Like manor houses, nunneries were usually located next to parish churches, and within the churches, the nuns often segregated themselves from laypeople by occupying an upper gallery, much as gentry families did in manorial chapels.[2] Gilchrist argues that in many ways nunneries echoed and reflected the life of aristocratic and gentry women of the period. Like these upper-class women, nuns lived secluded female lives, lives that by the late Middle Ages were increasingly defined by small households within the larger nunnery. Like upper-class women, nuns were primarily consumers rather than producers, both because of the small amount of land provided to nunneries and because most manual labor was done by men. However, nunneries also served as a space of power for women. Female-empowering imagery of female saints and the Virgin Mary within the female-only spaces of the nunnery reminded women of their religious potential, and the elaborated space of the refectory, where women could preach, served as a place of power.

Defining New Gender Roles

Monastic buildings are marked and segregated by gender because of the centrality of the rejection of traditional family and sexuality to the lives of men and women religious. They are thus a rich source for examining gender even in periods of relative stability in gender ideology. It is in periods of gender transformation, however, that we see the most sex segregation. When gender roles shift the definition of what constitutes masculinity or femininity, gender-segregated spaces can help to consolidate new gendered identities.

One era of shifting gender norms and cultural anxiety about gender is the late nineteenth and early twentieth centuries in the US. In this period, women were increasingly present in public space and the public sphere, as students in universities, shoppers and shopgirls in expanding downtown shopping districts, and workers in offices and factories. The transformation of female gender roles in the late nineteenth century was architecturally embodied by a series of spaces, including gender-segregated streetcars, department stores, women's

FIG. 3.3. The Ladies' Reading Room in the Buffalo Public Library resembles a parlor in many ways. The varied rugs on the floor, the multiple rocking chairs set at random angles, and the cozy but impressive fireplaces suggest a place of leisure. *The Buffalo Library and Its Building: Illustrated with Views* (Buffalo, NY: by the library, 1887), opp. 30.

waiting rooms, women's dining halls in hotels, and women's reading rooms, that allowed genteel women to make use of public spaces and the commercial downtown without overtly disturbing the ideology of separate spheres. This nineteenth-century ideology saw men and women as essentially different creatures, with men associated with the public sphere of work and politics and women associated with the private sphere of domesticity and the home. In keeping with the association of women and domestic space, spaces that accommodated women in public typically mimicked the domestic parlor both architecturally and through furnishing. They were also often enclosed and shielded from more heterogeneous public spaces.

Ladies' reading rooms in public libraries in the late nineteenth century, for example, were typically cozy rooms organized around a hearth, sometimes the only one in the building (figure 3.3). They were furnished with upholstered furniture, rocking chairs, and small tables, in contrast to the long tables and hard wooden chairs in grander

FIG. 3.4. In contrast to the ladies' reading room in figure 3.3, the Main Reading Room of the Detroit Public Library is a much larger, more formal and orderly space. The matching chairs and tables, lined up in precise rows; the bare parquet floor; and the cabinets of books mark this as an institutional space for serious reading. Photograph by Kenneth Clark, 1921, Library of Congress item 2014650177.

general reading rooms (figure 3.4). Potted plants and throw rugs further marked the space as feminine and domesticated, rather than institutional. They were often tucked away within the library as a whole, adjacent to library offices or children's reading rooms rather than the circulation desk or reference room, often with a ladies' restroom attached (figure 3.5). Furnishing ladies' readings rooms like parlors and hiding them away from more public parts of the library, especially the reading room, did not reflect women's desires, Abigail Van Slyck argues. Instead, ladies' reading rooms and their design reflected the desire of the male elite who were supporting libraries. Elite men wanted to have women in the libraries performing female respectability, thereby making the urban space of the library more orderly and polite. Van Slyck builds her argument on an extensive exploration of photographs, drawings, plans, and descriptions of libraries found in both national architectural and library journals and in the publications and annual reports

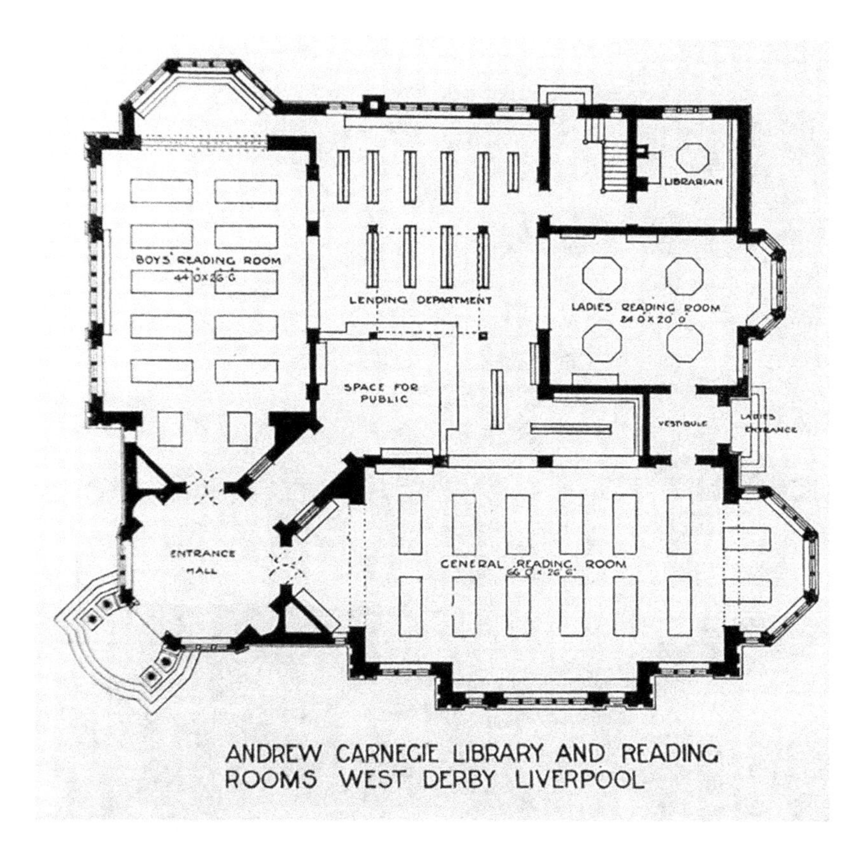

FIG. 3.5. The ladies' reading room in the Lister Drive Carnegie Library and Reading Rooms, Liverpool, UK, is separated from the general reading room by a vestibule, which can also be directly accessed through a discreet ladies' entrance. Thomas Shelmerdine, 1904, public domain, Wikimedia Commons.

of library associations. These sources allow her to find patterns in the design and furnishing of libraries. Comparing larger libraries with small libraries run by women's clubs in Western towns, Van Slyck shows that women-run spaces were more institutional in design than the ladies' reading rooms in large public libraries.[3]

While ladies' reading rooms, ladies' waiting rooms, and other parlor-like spaces appeared to reproduce Victorian gender ideology, they also helped to transform both women's lives and public understandings of gender. In part, they brought women into public spaces, including the mixed-gender, mixed-class spaces of the sidewalk and public transportation, as I discuss in more detail in chapter 4. More fundamentally, they helped remake the culture of public space, transforming it into a domesticated commercialized space which put a high value on both physical and moral comfort and was characterized by the sorting of people and spaces on the basis of class and racial lines.[4]

Even as the public sphere was being transformed into a more commercial and feminized space in the late nineteenth century, changes

FIG. 3.6. Masonic lodges constructed substantial buildings on the main streets of towns throughout North America, providing rental storefronts and offices as well as a central respectable location for the Lodge Hall. These buildings publicly express the permanence and propriety of Masons. No. 93, Main Street, Chardon, Ohio. Photograph by Chris Light, CC BY-SA 4.0 https://creativecommons.org/licenses/by-sa/4.0, Wikimedia Commons.

tied to corporate capitalism challenged models of masculine identity based on the workplace. New workplace hierarchies and machine technologies devalued the traditional skills and autonomy of artisans and made chance and social connections more important to upward mobility than hard work and skills. In addition, the growth of white-collar labor disconnected physical prowess from work, creating what many have argued was a crisis of masculinity and fueling social activities that encouraged manliness, including summer camps, big game hunting, and organized sports.[5] In American religion, shifts emphasized faith over doctrine, emotion over reason, a forgiving rather than a stern God, and the importance of mothers to their children's spiritual upbringing, changing the ways that both men and women understood their religious identities, and giving women more religious authority.[6]

In this context of challenges to masculine identities, all-male Masonic lodge rooms functioned as ritual spaces of masculinity. William Moore situates the enormous popularity of lodges in the late nineteenth

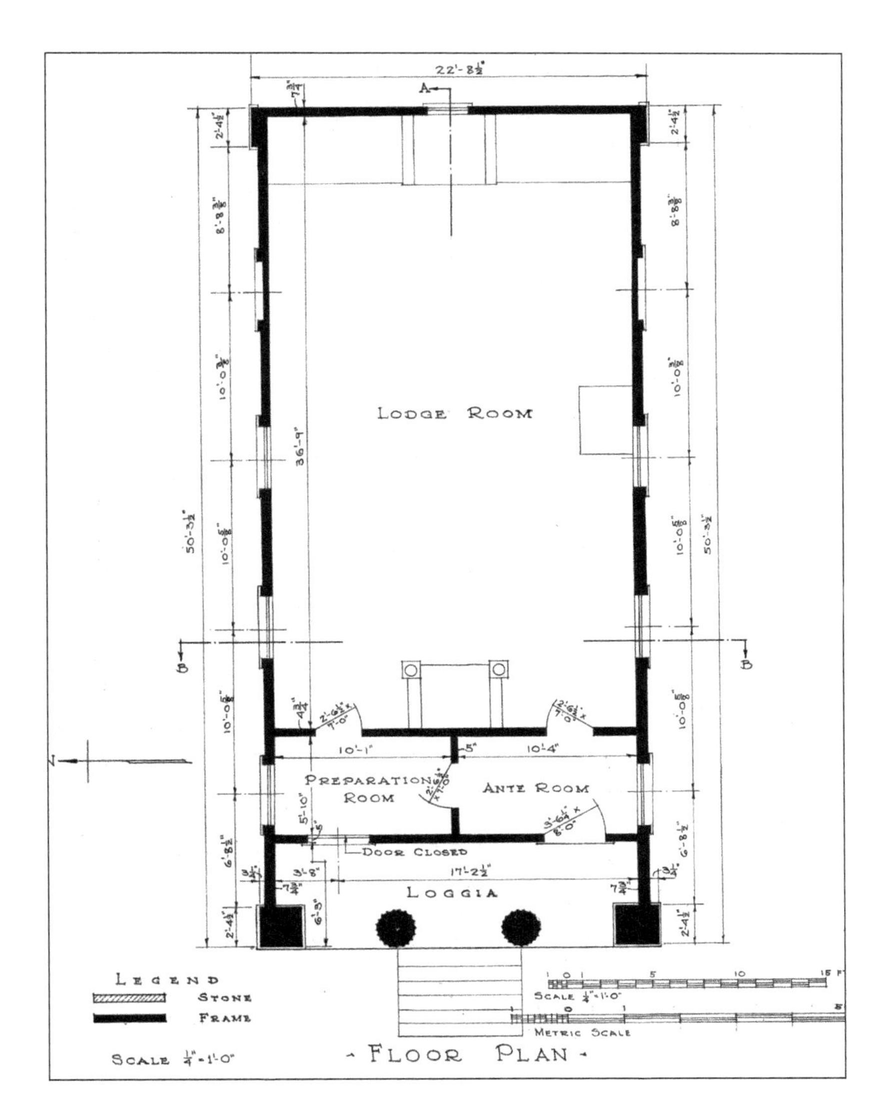

FIG. 3.7 On this plan of King Solomon's Lodge, Woodbury, Connecticut, we can see how the anteroom and preparation room provide a buffer between the ordinary world outside the lodge room and the sacred space of Masonic ritual. Detail of HABS CONN 3-WOO, 4, sheet 2 of 9.

century in the context of these changes in the workplace and in religion, both realms that had provided men with a sense of what it was to be a man. The space and ritual of the Masonic lodge set up both a clear and visible hierarchy based on the structure of traditional artisans' guilds and a spiritual experience akin to a male-only church, working to psychically counter these challenges to masculine identity. To understand how Masonic lodge rooms expressed and constructed masculinity, it is necessary to combine an attention to the physical structure of Masonic lodges with a nuanced exploration of their material culture, including furniture, and an understanding of how these spaces were used within Masonic ritual. Centering an analysis on ritual allows us to see how

FIG. 3.8. The interior space of the Masonic lodge is laid out to accommodate a carefully choreographed ritual. Each officer of the lodge sits at a prescribed location, and the elements of the room and their relationship to each other are the same in every lodge. Lodge of Entered Apprentices, Fellow Crafts, or Master Masons. Malcolm C. Duncan, *Duncan's Masonic Ritual and Monitor* (New York: Dick & Fitzgerald, 1866), 8.

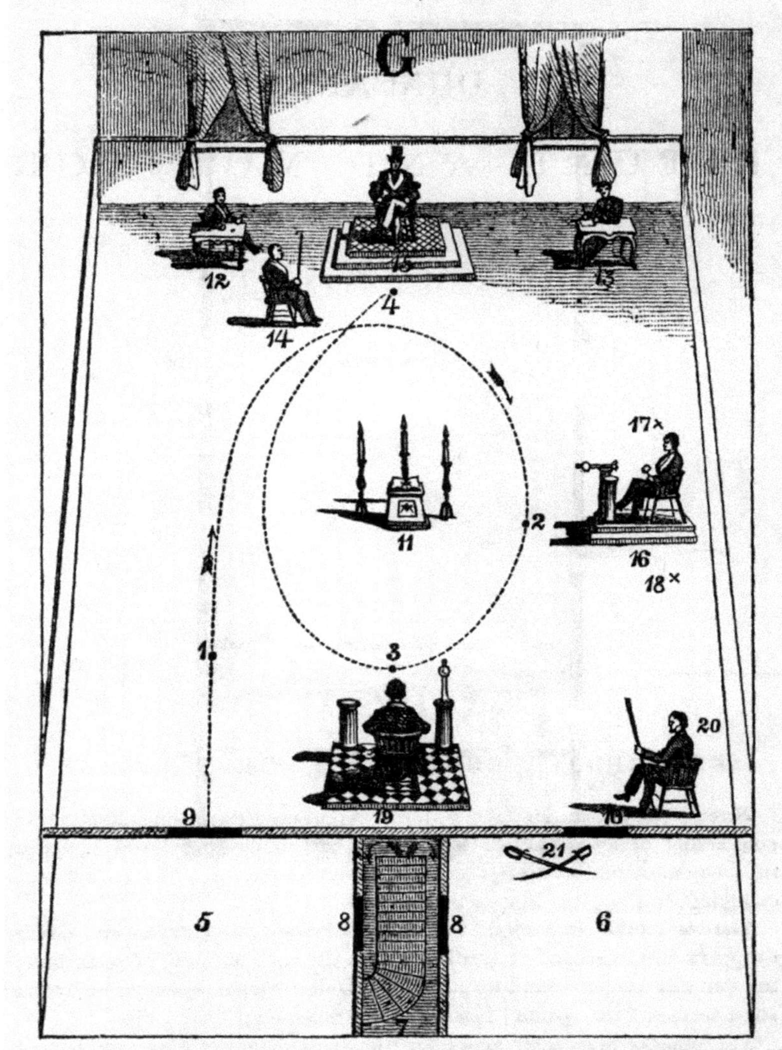

LODGE OF ENTERED APPRENTICES, FELLOW CRAFTS, OR MASTER MASONS.

1. Candidate prays. 2. First stop. 3. Second stop. 4. Third stop. 5. Room where candidates are prepared. 6. Ante-room where members enter the lodge. 7. Hall. 8. Doors. 9. Door through which candidates are admitted into the lodge. 10. Door through which members enter. 11. Altar. 12. Treasurer. 13. Secretary. 14. Senior Deacon. 15. Worshipful Master. 16. Junior Warden. 17 and 18. Stewards. 19. Senior Warden. 20. Junior Deacon. 21. Tyler.

the architecture and furnishings worked to reconstruct middle-class masculinity.

Masonic lodge rooms are typically located on the upper floor of a substantial building in a central location in a town or city (figure 3.6). The building speaks to the power and status of the Masons and provides both rental income and a centrally located meeting space physi-

FIG. 3.9 East Blue Lodge Room, Masonic Temple, Detroit, c. 1910. The tall gothic chairs at the end of the room and to the right are for the Worshipful Master and other dignitaries, while the bench seating is for the rest of the lodge members. Detroit Publishing Company photograph collection, Library of Congress, http://hdl.loc.gov/loc.pnp/det.4a20483.

cally removed from the ordinary world of the street. Nonexistent or permanently veiled windows helped to highlight the separation of the sacred space of the meeting room, which was understood as a simulacrum of Solomon's Temple. Donning Masonic aprons helped to mark the passage from the profane into the Temple, as did the presence of an anteroom watched over by a sword-wielding lodge officer known as the Tyler (figure 3.7). Decoration that featured Masonic symbols, Masonic pillars, and a wide range of historical design references, including the Gothic and Egyptian revival styles, further marked this sacred space as special and referenced the idea that freemasonry had existed since the beginning of Western civilization.[7]

The Masonic lodge room is organized to accommodate and highlight the ritual it contains. It is a long rectangle with a high ceiling, bisected by two axes that intersect at a central altar (figure 3.8). The longer primary axis runs from the letter G on the wall (representing both G and

Geometry), through the master and the altar, and ends at the senior warden. The secondary axis runs from the junior warden through the altar to the far wall. The officers at the terminals of these axes sit on tall, monumental chairs, which combine with their ritual clothing to mark their places within a strict hierarchy. The rest of the members sit on identical chairs arrayed along the walls, such that members are visible to each other and there is no visible hierarchy among the members who are not officers (figure 3.9). Every person, including the officers, is equidistant to the altar, showing a direct relationship to God, not one mediated through clergy.[8] The organization of the lodge room, its decoration, its furnishings, and its relationship to the rest of the building all work together with the ritual to create a space dedicated to a masculine identity characterized by corporate identity and hierarchy.

Shaping Gender

Masonic lodge rooms helped men construct a sense of themselves as Masons at a time when their sense of masculinity defined through work was in flux. Lodge rooms were used by the same people who shaped

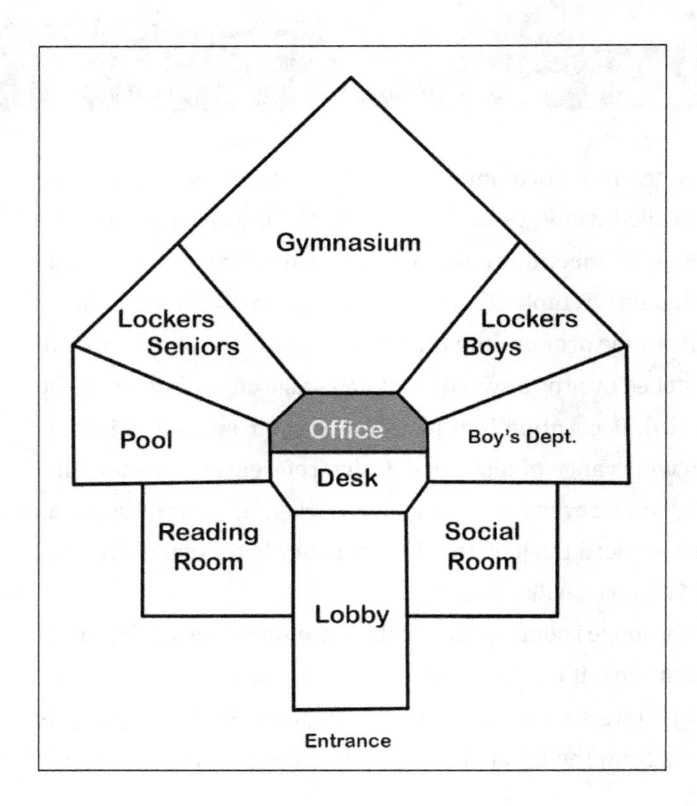

FIG. 3.10. In the ideal YMCA, all the spaces and the young men in them are constantly being supervised by YMCA officers. This diagrammatic plan of ideal supervision in YMCAs from 1915 shows the panoptic position of the front desk and office, from which entrants through the lobby can be screened and the spaces of athletic activity and edification can be watched over. Drawing by Jessica Sewell based on image in Louis Jallade, *The Association Building* (New York: Association Press, 1913).

FIG. 3.11. The 1869 New York City YMCA library is a grand space, with soaring ceilings, excellent lighting, decorative and substantial shelving, and well-dressed patrons. *Harpers Weekly*, Dec. 11, 1869, 785.

them, but most single-gender spaces are not. For example, in the post–Civil War era, YMCAs were created by older elite White Christian men for the use of a much broader male population, particularly young middle- and working-class men. Through YMCAs, elite businessmen sought to shape a virtuous, Christian masculine identity in working-class and newly white-collar men, in part by offering them clean lodging and entertainment to compete with saloons and urban vice. In downtown branches in major cities, early YMCAs offered libraries, parlors, and gymnasiums to would-be self-made men. In her study of YMCAs, Paula Lupkin argues that the creators of the 1869 New York YMCA and other downtown YMCAs used elite masculine spaces and paternalistic oversight to encourage desirable moral and middle-class male behavior. YMCA designs combined panoptic surveillance, centered on the reception room with its front desk, with spaces of edification and refinement (figure 3.10). For example, the New York YMCA library provided an opportunity for young men to educate themselves in a space reminiscent of elite private libraries (figure 3.11). Surrounding classrooms and a grand lecture hall provided further space for education. A suite of parlors encouraged young men to civilize themselves and to prepare for their role as paterfamiliases. Within YMCA parlors, as in both private and public parlors that men shared with women, young men had to behave with their best comportment. While the parlor was

FIG. 3.12. The young men doing calisthenics at the Central Queens branch of the YMCA, New York City, in 1926 strengthened their bodies through a group activity that prized conformity and precision. University of Minnesota Libraries, Kautz Family YMCA Archives, https://umedia.lib.umn.edu/item/p16022coll261:2674.

usually associated with femininity, it was also a space of male privilege, expressive of the power of the male head of household.[9]

The 1869 New York YMCA also included a basement gymnasium, where young white-collar workers could strengthen and discipline their bodies, counteracting the negative effects of office work and quelling the desire for less moral bodily pleasures. Later in the nineteenth century, gymnasium spaces and swimming pools took up more and more of YMCA buildings, replacing large meeting halls and parlors and filling up annexes, reflecting the growth of "muscular Christianity." Athletic spaces served as a means of building character, readying young men for the discipline of corporate culture through a combination of regimentation (in group calisthenics, for example) and competition (figure 3.12). They also helped the YMCA compete with public amusements for the attention of young men. Beginning in the late

FIG. 3.13. In contrast to the White YMCAs, the Colored YMCA branch on West 53rd Street in New York City in 1901 had significantly more cramped spaces. The fixtures, furniture, and decoration of this reading room are expressive of respectability, as are the focus on reading and the men's suits. University of Minnesota Libraries, Kautz Family YMCA Archives, https://umedia.lib.umn.edu/item/p16022coll261:2642.

1880s, YMCAs began to offer rooms to rent, thus ensuring themselves of steady revenue while overseeing all aspects of young men's lives.[10]

Opening separate branches downtown and in Black and working-class neighborhoods as well as industrial and railroad branches across the US, the YMCA worked to shape young men in class-specific ways. Spaces in White, middle-class YMCAs were often grand, offering young men a glimpse of an elite world they might strive towards. In contrast, YMCAs serving working-class men focused on providing a range of services to uplift working men and provide them with alternatives to commercial amusements. Railroad YMCAs were the first to provide dormitories and restaurants; and gymnasiums, bowling alleys, game rooms, and other wholesome amusements provided an alternative to saloons. YMCAs focused on working men also provided reading rooms complete with trade magazines and vocational training.[11] Many YMCAs serving

FIG. 3.14. The Chicago YMCA hotel guest rooms on this circa 1930 postcard vary in size, but they each provide a dresser, bed, table, and at least one chair in a compact space quite like university dorm rooms.

Black men had cramped, oversubscribed spaces (figure 3.13), although Black-run YMCAs were boosted after 1910, when Julius Rosenwald, president of Sears, pledged to provide $25,000 to any Black YMCA that could raise $75,000.[12] Class segregation was even present within YMCAs serving White middle-class men, such as the 1894 Chicago YMCA. In this YMCA's gym facilities, ordinary members and more elite businessmen were segregated in the locker rooms, where elite members had private lockers, showers, club rooms, and Turkish baths.

College dormitories serve a similar function to YMCAs in shaping young people, and YMCA rooms were remarkably similar to dorm rooms of the same period (figure 3.14). Carla Yanni uses a comparative technique in her examination of college dormitories, which she studies using a range of sources such as buildings, plans, and photographs, including photographs showing how spaces were used. Contemporary writing about dormitories and coeducation, letters, and other archival sources provide her with more detail about the ideas underlying dormitory design and how dormitories were used and experienced. Dormitories were built for women beginning in the late nineteenth century at coed colleges, especially public universities in the midwestern US.

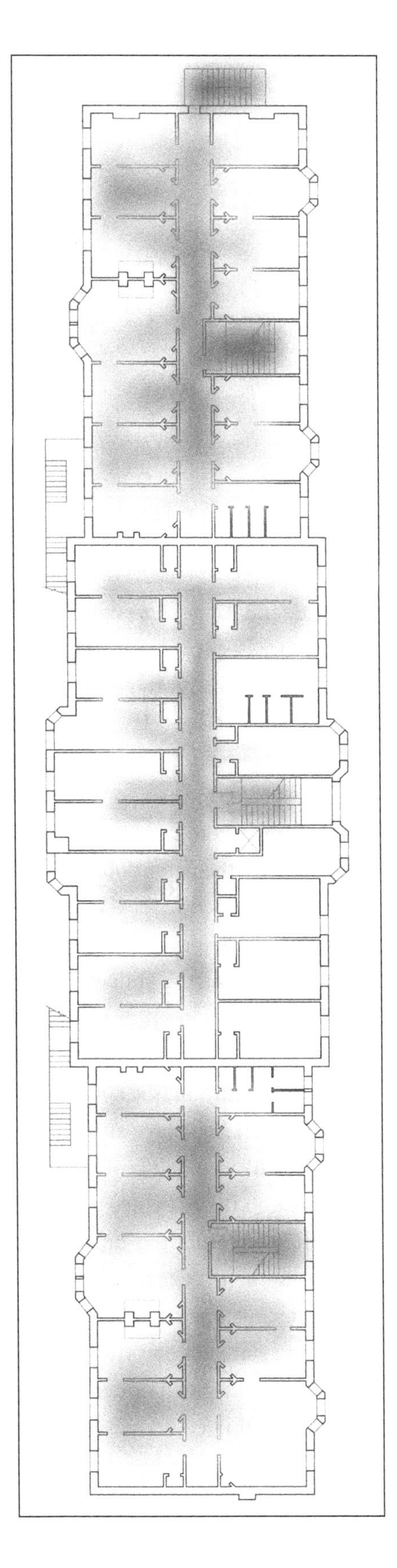

FIG. 3.15. This plan of the second floor of a women's dorm at the University of Chicago shows rooms along a double-loaded corridor, accessed by a shared staircase. The coming and going of women students and their guests is easily surveilled by controlling access to the staircase. This is quite distinct from the men's dorm in figure 3.17. Plan of second floor of Green Hall, University of Chicago, 1893–1898, Henry Ives Cobb, architect. Drawing by Tabi Summers.

FIG. 3.16. Ridenbaugh Hall, a women's dormitory at the University of Idaho, is typical in its single entrance and comparative lack of openness at the ground floor, ensuring women students' rooms are shielded from those outside and facilitating surveillance. 1910 Postcard of Ridenbaugh Hall, University of Idaho. Steve Shook from Moscow, Idaho, USA, CC BY 2.0 Wikimedia Commons.

These dorms typically provided private single rooms along double-loaded corridors on the upper floors and shared grand dining and entertaining rooms on the first floor (figure 3.15). Women's dorms were entered from a single central entrance, which facilitated surveillance of women's coming and going and limited guest access (figure 3.16). Dorm architects refer to this type of plan as the double-loaded corridor plan. They differed from dorms for men in the provision of grand rooms for entertaining, the attention to privacy, and the single entrance. Men's dorms were much more likely to have multiple entrances, each leading to a staircase that served stacked dorm rooms, a type known by dorm planners as the stairway or entryway plan (figure 3.17). This difference in floor plan communicates that collegiate women needed to be sheltered and protected, while collegiate men had significantly more freedom. In addition, the large entertainment spaces in women's dorms served as a space where students could practice entertaining for their future as cultured housewives and where male students could be civilized through the presence of women.[13]

While they adopted dormitories in the early twentieth century, in the nineteenth century many women's colleges instead made use of smaller cottages to house female students (figure 3.18). As Helen Horowitz relates in her study of women's colleges and their architecture, Smith College's founders feared that students who were housed in a single building could become too separate from conventional family life and might reject it in favor of a life of the mind and, potentially, of lesbianism. Domestic houses or cottages, in contrast, would help

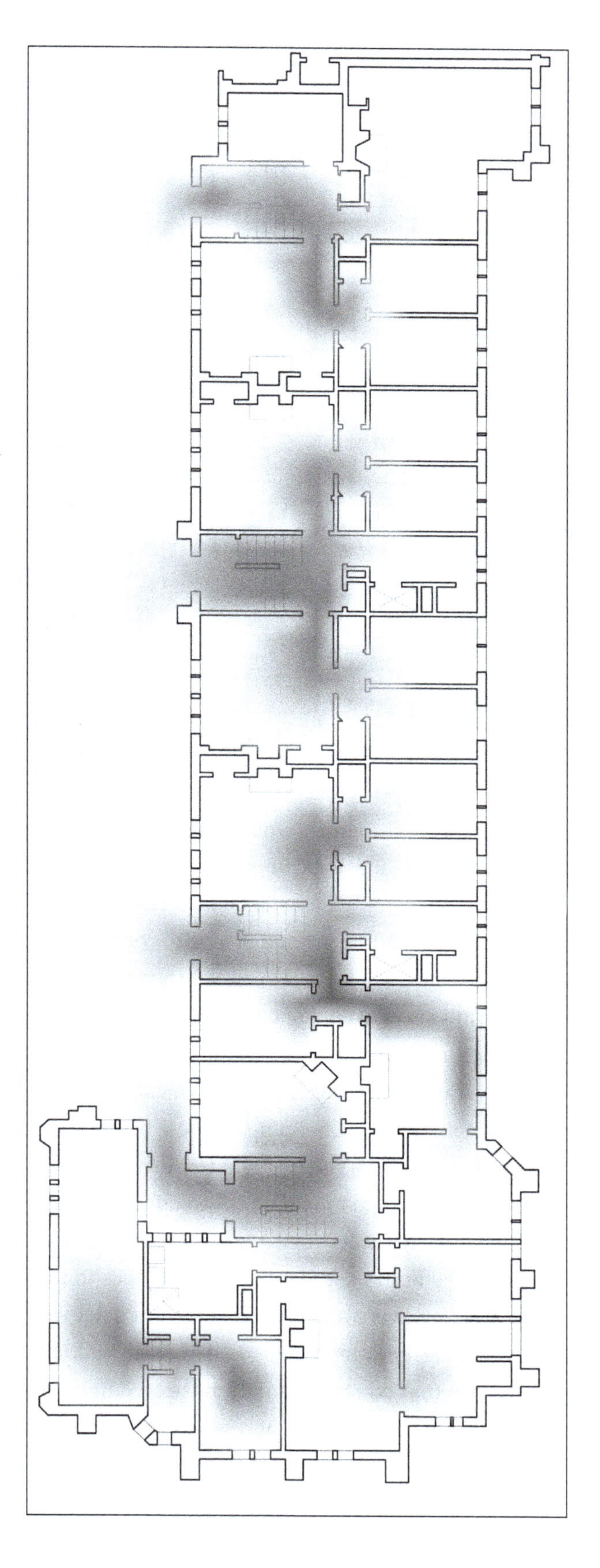

FIG. 3.17. In contrast to the women's dorm in figure 3.15, in this men's dorm at Yale University, dorm rooms are organized around multiple staircases, and students can come and go without central surveillance. In addition, the rooms are organized as shared suites, while women's dorms are more typically individual cells, as in figure 3.15. This is reflective of the idea that women have more need of privacy. Portion of Calhoun College (now Grace Hopper College), Yale University, 1932–1933, John Russell Pope, architect. Drawing by Tabi Summers.

FIG. 3.18. This "cottage" dormitory at Smith College has the appearance of a grand house for a single family. This domestic space, complete with first-floor parlors and a live-in "lady in charge" functioning as a house mother, mimics family living, preparing women students for potential domestic futures while also making women's education appear less threatening to gender norms. Hatfield House, Smith College. Postcard, c. 1914.

preserve women students' "womanliness." The houses were large domestic structures, housing from thirty-two to fifty students, along with a "lady-in-charge" and a female faculty member, who each had rooms on the ground floor. The ground floor also contained a parlor or parlors and a large dining room. While all but the first of Smith's houses were purpose-built specifically to house large numbers of students, their exteriors and the organization of the first floor meant that they felt more like family homes than dormitories. Tall gables helped to minimize the perceived volume of the building, while a broad and welcoming porch softened the building's relationship to the outside and signaled its domesticity. The cottage model was also adopted at other women's colleges, including Wellesley (figure 3.19). The cottages at women's colleges communicated both to students and to visitors to their campuses that women students were and should be tied to a domestic ideal. The image of domestic femininity embodied in these buildings helped to work against fears that education might unsex women, making them more masculine.[14] As coeducation and women's college education became more common in the early twentieth century, the domestic symbolism of cottages became less essential, and many women's colleges added

FIG. 3.19. Wellesley College also followed the cottage model, housing students in dorms that looked like large houses. With Fiske Cottage, the front section of the dorm with its sheltering porch appears very domestic. However, its institutional nature is revealed by the railings along the mansard roof and the large addition to the rear. Postcard, c. 1906.

dormitories with a collegiate feel. For example, Wellesley's Quadrangle, built between 1904 and 1915, is a variation on collegiate gothic, with floors of rooms architecturally distinct from the public rooms in the towers (figure 3.20).[15]

Gender Dichotomies in the Built Environment

In addition to single-gender spaces, we can see a dichotomous understanding of gender built into many public edifices, including schools and public baths with entrances and facilities separated by gender. Public restrooms are ubiquitous markers of gender dichotomy in contemporary public spaces. They are typically labelled with outline figures of gendered bodies and are often referred to as ladies' or men's rooms, names that only reference gender, not use. The design and placement of public bathrooms, as well as their presence or absence in a given setting, communicate about culturally prescribed gender roles in public space. When public restrooms were first built in European and American cities in the nineteenth century, they only provided urinals for men. Men could also often use facilities in saloons, spaces that were not open

FIG. 3.20. Unlike earlier cottage dorms like Fiske Cottage (figure 3.19), the Quadrangle at Wellesley College is a clearly institutional building, making use of the Collegiate Gothic style visible at campuses like Princeton, Yale, and the University of Chicago. The use of this style signals that women's education should be treated as equivalent in value to men's and that Wellesley should be considered equivalent to its masculine Ivy League counterparts. Postcard, c. 1930.

to women. The lack of toilet facilities for women expressed the idea that women did not belong in public space and made it physically difficult for women to spend extensive periods of time in public, as they were constrained by what bathroom scholars call the "urinary leash." The contemporary provision of restrooms primarily within private shops and restaurants further constrains access to the public realm by race and class.[16] When toilet facilities for elite White women were provided, as in hotels and department stores in the late nineteenth century, they often were designed with an outer room for resting, putting on makeup, and otherwise preparing themselves to go back out into public. Women's rooms of this sort provide layers of privacy between the act of elimination and the shared public realm.[17] In contrast, many men's toilet facilities, particularly in the nineteenth century, barely shielded the center of men's bodies (figure 3.21). Most recently, the Uritrottoir urinals provided in Paris, which resemble trash bins, barely shield men's privates, while simultaneously providing highly visible facilities in prominent locations for men only.[18]

This attention to privacy for females is notable in girls' summer

FIG. 3.21 The urinals built in Paris in the nineteenth century were designed for minimal privacy. A passerby can immediately see whether the urinal is occupied, and this constant surveillance encouraged users to urinate quickly and leave, nearly eliminating the possibility of sexual activity. The stall is also easily hosed down. Urinals like this mark public space as men's territory, and no facilities were provided for women. Parisian 3 Stall Urinal, photograph by Charles Marville, c. 1865, collection of State Library Victoria.

camp bathrooms in the mid-twentieth-century US (figure 3.22). These typically provided separate shower stalls as well as private toilet stalls, while boys' summer camp bathrooms had a gang shower and gang urinals (figure 3.23). In addition, while girls' bathrooms had a single entrance, boys' bathrooms typically had multiple doors. Summer camp bathrooms not only signal a gender difference in terms of privacy, but also in terms of cleanliness. Showerheads greatly outnumbered toilets for girls, while the boys had two toilets for every showerhead. Boys were also typically provided with a large shared sink for washing, while girls more often had individual washbasins; and girls were also provided space specifically for washing clothes, which was not part of boys' washrooms.[19] By comparing gendered bathrooms we can see how

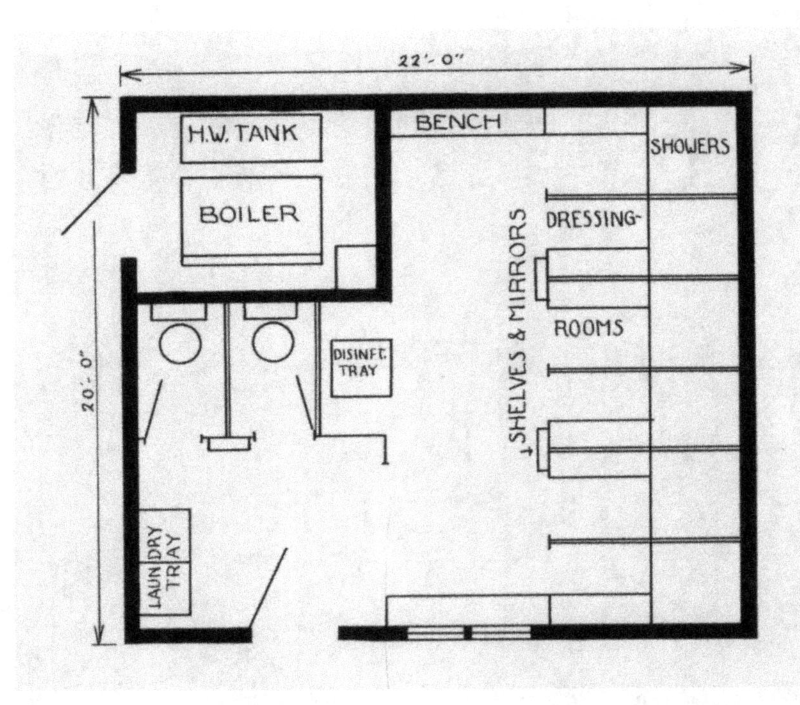

FIG. 3.22. Camp Fire Girls Shower House plan, c. 1945. This washhouse provides six shower stalls, each with a dressing room, and just two toilet stalls. The shower space takes up over half of the building. This reflects the idea that women and girls are or should be fastidious in their cleanliness and require privacy in showering, dressing, and eliminating. This design also encourages bodily modesty. Adapted from Camp Fire Girls, *When You Plan Your Camp* (New York: Camp Fire Girls, 1946).

design decisions that might not be notable on their own become significant when contrasted with designs for another gender.

Why Study Single-Gender Spaces?

Single-gender spaces, because of the explicit nature of their gendering, can help us to see the particular, often exaggerated ways that gender is expressed in the built environment in a given cultural and historical context. This can help us to see gender in other parts of the built environment, such as when we recognize a gendered design vocabulary from a single-gender space being used elsewhere to communicate similar gendered meanings. Comparing parallel spaces for men and women, such as monasteries and dorm rooms, gives us the opportunity to recognize what aspects of design are reflective of gender differences. It allows us to see, for example, that choosing to design a dorm building with a single entrance is not necessarily gender neutral, but rather expresses the desire to keep female students more protected and controlled.

All the studies discussed in this chapter begin from the buildings themselves, whether accessed through fieldwork, through archaeologi-

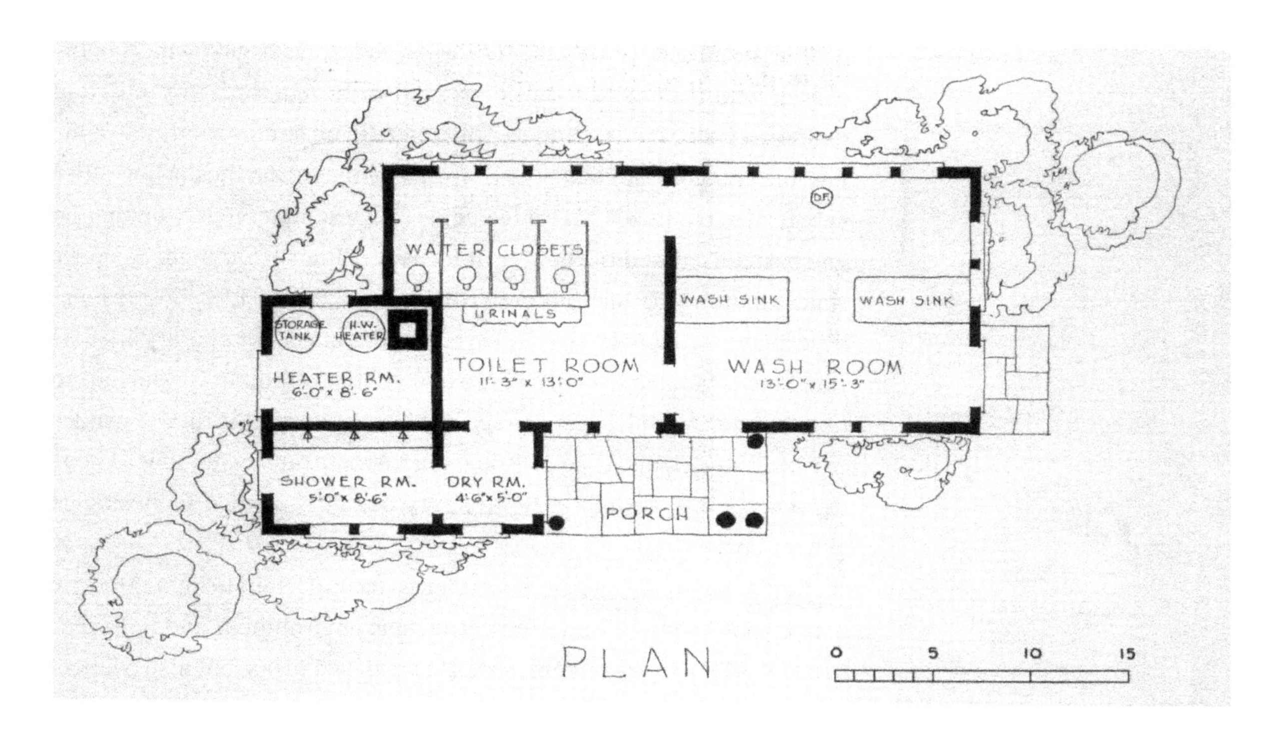

cal digs, through published or archival drawings and photographs, or through textual descriptions. Photographs and descriptions enrich our understanding of the nature of a place by providing glimpses of material culture, showing us how a space was furnished and hinting at how it was used. But in order to recognize both that a space is gendered and what models of gender it enacts, we need to go beyond the exploration of the physical fabric of buildings. We can learn more about how a space was intended to be used and the ideas that it encapsulates by looking at the written record, such as the publications of YMCA and Masonic organizations and library professionals, as well as other papers of the clients, designers, and decision-makers shaping the space. Paying attention to who shaped a space and who used it is essential for understanding to what extent a building was intended to enforce and inculcate ways of understanding and enacting gender. While some of the ideas of late nineteenth-century manhood expressed through Masonic halls and YMCAs are similar, Masonic halls more directly reflect the desires of their users, while YMCAs express, at least in part, the desires of elite men for moral, disciplined workers. These questions of power matter.

Future work on single-gender spaces will be enriched by an explicitly intersectional approach, and an approach that explicitly addresses

FIG. 3.23. In contrast to the girls' washhouse in figure 3.22, this YMCA camp washhouse for boys provides a much smaller space for showering, with no private stalls. The floorspace for the showers is less than half the space of the toilet room, which includes urinals as well as toilet stalls. This design suggests that boys are less concerned with cleanliness and demands a lack of bodily modesty from its users. Plan of Unit Washhouse for a YMCA Camp, John A. Ledlie, ed., *Layout, Building Designs and Equipment for Y.M.C.A. Camps* (New York: Young Man's Christian Association, 1946), 48.

gender as culturally contingent. It is key to always begin by thoroughly examining the particularities of gender, class, age, sexuality, etc. that define a space that we understand as male or female, and not to allow the category of gender to erase these particularities or for other categories to entirely override gender. For example, much writing on gay bars (discussed in chapter 4) focuses primarily on them as queer spaces, but the distinctions between bars used exclusively by gay men, by lesbians, by transexuals, and by a broader queer community are distinctions of gender as well as of sexuality. It also remains important to understand any single-gender space in the context of the mixed-gender world around it, and especially anxieties about transformations in gender, class, race, sexuality, etc. that are being responded to by single-gender spaces.

Exploring single-gender spaces gives us important insight into how gender has been built into the vernacular environment and how vernacular architecture not only reflects gendered ideas, but also participates in their construction and reproduction. However, focusing only on single-gender spaces gives us a very partial view of the relationship between gender and the vernacular built environment. Single-gender spaces are rare and usually tightly conscribed by race and class, so give us a limited picture, and one that usually reflects the gender ideology of the most powerful. Limiting our focus to single-gender spaces can also imply that only these spaces are gendered, leaving the majority of the built environment unscrutinized. Just as the growth of Whiteness studies pushes us to interrogate how race is constructed through the entire built environment, not only those spaces that are explicitly racialized as non-White, a critical perspective on gender and vernacular architecture demands that we explore how gender is part of the entire built environment, including both single-gender and mixed-gender spaces for all classes, ethnicities, and races.

4

MIXED-GENDER SPACES

Most built spaces are mixed gender, although we may not always look at them through a gendered lens. As this chapter argues, mixed-gender vernacular architecture both reflects and enforces heterosexual gendered ideologies. As we have seen in the previous chapter, single-gender spaces articulate the social definition of a gendered identity, painting a picture of the nature of masculinity or femininity at a particular place and time. Mixed-gender spaces tell us about gendered roles and identities in relationship to each other and also serve as a physical embodiment of social structures such as kinship and prestige that help to define gendered identities and roles. Nearly any mixed-gender space could potentially be read for gender, but those that are entangled with social structures that create and reinforce gender are often the most fruitful to explore. Because structures of kinship are the most intimately tied to gender, houses are an excellent place to start an exploration of mixed-gender space. This chapter will then move on to look at how gender is also a fruitful lens for examining many public spaces, using the examples of workplaces, restaurants, and commercial streets.

House and Gender

Houses reflect the organization of people and activities within a household and therefore express important categories of gender, age, and relationship. We can read houses for cultural ideas about gender, kinship, and age because they both embody cultural categories and create a frame for activities that enact those categories. It is common for anthropologists, whose object of study is culture, to explore space and architecture not so much as things in themselves, but as material culture, embedded elements of a lived culture, expressing and enacting ideas that are also present in everyday practices, language, ritual, etc. Looking at vernacular architecture in a broad cultural context allows us to see the association between structural relationships, which create "social maps" of people and activities, and how they are "realized 'on the ground' by the placing of individuals in space."[1]

GENDER IN NON-WESTERN HOUSES

While contemporary houses in the global North are often organized primarily around the distinctions between children and adults and between communal and private spaces, the categories of male and female have been dominant in other traditions and remain highly salient in the West as well. For example, among the Marakwet of Kenya, the male/female duality is a dominant symbolic structure, used to express all kinds of conflicts and distinctions. The feminist anthropologist Henrietta L. Moore argues that this duality is expressed through the family compound. Traditionally a Marakwet household lives in an enclosed compound with a male house and a female house facing each other along a north-south axis (figure 4.1). The woman's house is the space of cooking, and the ash created by the cooking fire as well as the chaff from preparing grain that she has grown are female substances that remain on that side of the compound. They are mirrored on the opposite side by animal dung, connected with men and the task of animal herding. Even when the duality male house / female house is translated in practice into sleeping house / cooking house, the dual structure, and its tie to gender duality, remains.[2]

Moore's analysis is based on her own embodied ethnographic research and previous ethnographic studies, which give her a broader historical and geographical context for her highly localized fieldwork. She explores compound structure in the context of lived experience, showing how compounds change through the lifetime of a household, how traditional organizational principles are translated into modern housing forms, and how the ways individuals live within the household enact conceptions of gender. The physical form of the house, she ar-

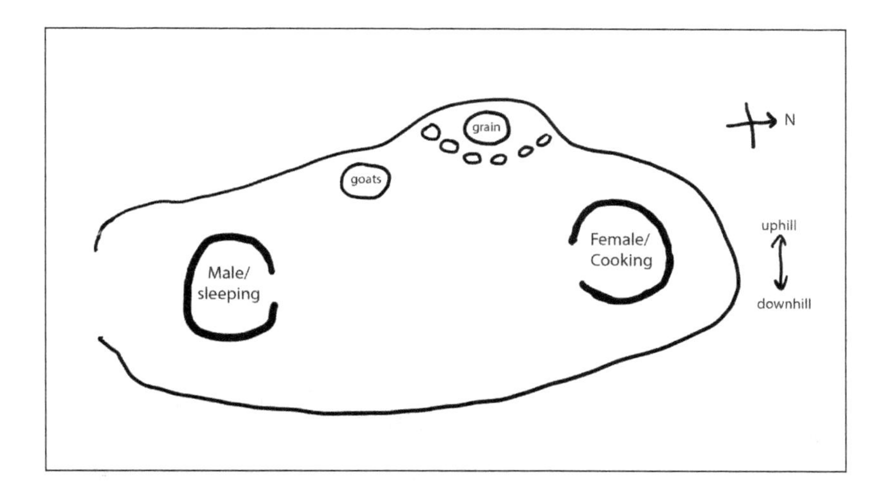

FIG. 4.1. In Marakwet compounds in Kenya, space is organized by gender. The woman's house, the granary, and ash and chaff, materials associated with women, are on the north end of the compound. The man's house, the goathouse, and animal dung, a material associated with men, are on the south. While both men and women often use both houses, conceptually space is defined by gender. Drawing by Jessica Sewell based on Henrietta Moore, *Space, Text, and Gender: An Anthropological Study of the Marakwet of Kenya* (New York: Guilford Press, 1996), figure 17.

gues, functions both to support those behaviors and to express gender structures.

While we can read a house plan as a map of gender and other categories of difference underlying kinship and the household, it is useful to also think of it as a technology of gender which actively shapes practice. In her study of gender in Ming and Qing dynasty (1368–1911) China, anthropologist Francesca Bray examines the vernacular courtyard house as one technology "giving shape and meaning to the lives of women," along with the weaving of cloth and the producing of children.[3] While she asks anthropological questions about broad cultural rules and rituals, because her subject is historical, she uses largely textual sources, particularly historical etiquette, household management, and builders' guides, to explore the meanings and use of traditional Chinese courtyard houses.

The household contained by a late imperial Chinese house is multigenerational and patrilinear, consisting of a male head of household, his wife or wives, and his sons and their wives. Its design and the ways of living within it express and enable the hierarchies of generation, age, gender, and status that organize not just the household but the culture as a whole. In neo-Confucian thought, the household was a microcosm of imperial power, such that the emperor functioned structurally as the father of China.[4] This parallel is visible in the design of the imperial palace, which is the Chinese courtyard house writ large and follows the same principles of organization and marking of status. For

FIG. 4.2. Central hall of a traditional courtyard house on Shantang Jie in Suzhou, China, which is used as an ancestral hall. The tall, elaborated roof and the short staircase leading to this slightly elevated room mark it as the highest status place in the compound. Photograph by Jessica Sewell, 2015.

example, in a vernacular house, the status of each room is marked not only by position, but also by height. The most important room has a higher and more elaborated roof, and its floor is often raised higher as well (figure 4.2). The extremely elaborated roofs and punishingly high staircases marking the most important ceremonial rooms in the Forbidden City use this same principle to mark their supremely high status (figure 4.3). The marking of status by elements of the house was seen by Chinese philosophers as crucially important to keeping social order by reminding everyone of their place within the hierarchy; the medieval *Carpenter's Canon* warns, "the rear hall, main hall, corridors, and triple gate may increase only gradually in height, since only then do sons and grandsons know their rank; and does not the younger aspire to the older's place."[5]

The Chinese courtyard house consists of halls arranged orthogonally around one or a series of courtyards and enclosed by a wall into a compound (figure 4.4). It is oriented to the cardinal directions, with the entrance gate to the walled enclosure, and the principal east-west rooms

FIG. 4.3 Hall of Supreme Harmony, Forbidden City, Beijing, China. This hall is centered east-west within the complex, faces south, and is significantly higher than the other buildings within the Forbidden City. The elaborated roof further emphasizes its height and thus the elevated status of the building. The very long staircase reminds all those climbing it of their low status in comparison to the emperor. Photograph by Jessica Sewell, 2013.

that parallel it, facing to the south. These east-west rooms are the highest status within the ensemble and contain public and ritual spaces. The north-south rooms mirror each other. These rooms are lower status and used for sleeping quarters and storage, with those on the east higher status than those on the west. Enclosure is an important aspect of the house, marking the distinction between family and outside, embodying the centrality of family as a category in Chinese neo-Confucian thought. The single gate further expressed the unity of the family under patriarchal rule, as the *Carpenter's Canon* argued that in a house with two gates "there will be no love between father and son."[6] The importance of the patriarchal line is also expressed through the placement of the ancestral shrine in the highest status space in the house and through the daily rituals honoring the ancestors. The same principles of organization were used in all scales of households, such that even in a one-room house, spaces were differentiated by furniture and use, and the ancestral shrine held the highest status role and sat in the center, facing south.

The use of the Chinese courtyard house enacts a separation of and differentiation between genders as well as hierarchy between male members of the household. The complementarity and hierarchy between the genders is expressed in multiple ways. For example, for the ritual honoring the ancestors, women enter the main hall on the west, in order of rank and age, while men enter on the east, the higher status side. Most significantly, women are associated with the interior spaces, to which in elite families they were largely confined, while men are associated with the outer world. While men and women shared

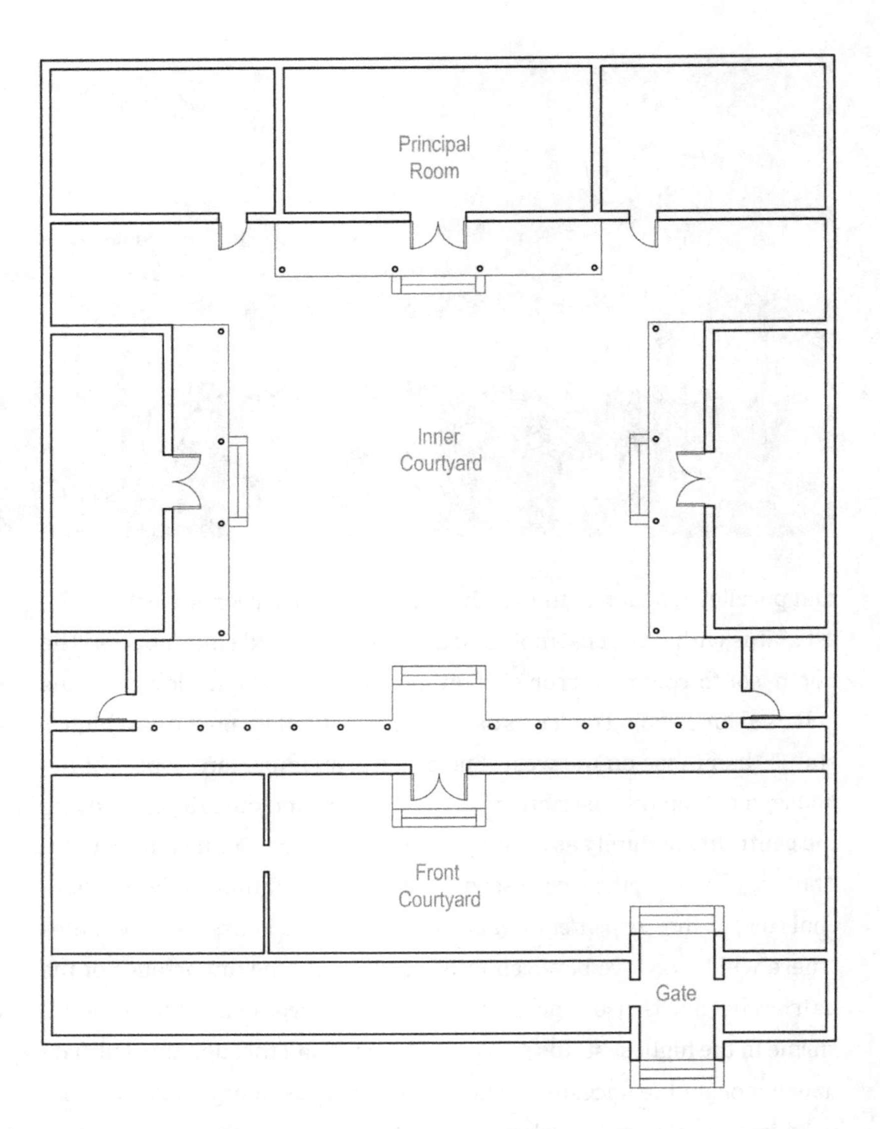

FIG. 4.4. Chinese courtyard houses can have one or several courtyards but always follow the same organizational rules. The most important room is centrally located and opens to the south, and the compound is only accessible through one door, which is never on axis. Plan of siheyuan (Chinese courtyard house), drawn by Tabi Summers.

FIG. 4.5. (*facing page*) The spaces for the elite family occupying this nineteenth-century English row house are segregated by gender, with the ground floor dining room and library (coded with horizontal lines) dominated by men and the first-floor drawing rooms (coded with diagonal lines) dominated by women. "Design for a Row of London Houses," Robert Kerr, *The Gentleman's House, or How to Plan English Residences* (London: John Murray, 1865), plate 44. Spaces coded by the author, indicating gender of elite residents.

bedrooms for sleeping, men were expected to spend the day outside or doing business in the outer courtyard, while women remained largely in the inner courtyard and in the bedrooms, which were understood as theirs to control. Each woman's room was furnished with the goods from her dowry, including a marriage bed and a locked chest which only she could open.

GENDER IN WESTERN HOUSES

The gendered nature of the traditional Chinese courtyard house, or any house, is only visible in the context of cultural rules about its use and, ideally, evidence of actual use, which can be found through

BASEMENT.
(OFFICES)

GROUND FLOOR.
(DINING ROOM &c)

FIRST FLOOR.
(DRAWING ROOMS)

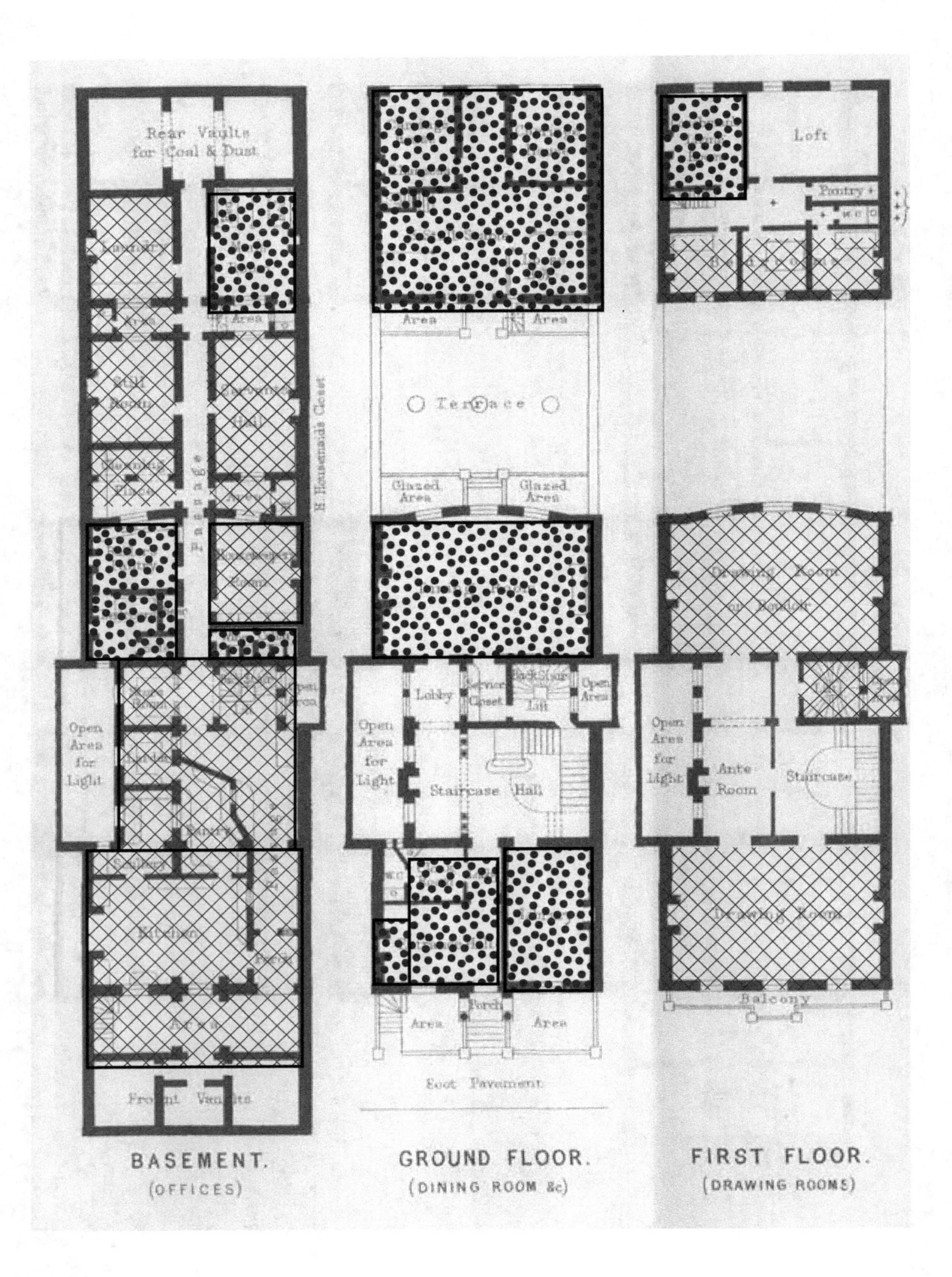

Rear Vaults for Coal & Dust
Area
Area
H Housemaids Closet
Open Area for Light
Front Vaults
BASEMENT.
(OFFICES)
Area
Area
Terrace
Glazed Area
Glazed Area
Lobby
Service Closet
Back Stair
Lift
Open Area
Open Area for Light
Staircase Hall
Porch
Area
Area
Foot Pavement
GROUND FLOOR.
(DINING ROOM &c)
Loft
Pantry
W.C
Open Area for Light
Ante Room
Staircase
Balcony
FIRST FLOOR.
(DRAWING ROOMS)

ethnography, interviews, prescriptive literature, and various sources that describe life within a house. These cultural rules, examined in combination with the house itself, allow us to see ways that rules of gender are interlinked with other cultural norms and embodied in the everyday life shaped by a house. In the case of the US and the United Kingdom in the nineteenth and twentieth centuries, scholars have explored how the ideal of the house as a haven apart from the world of work, rules of privacy, specialization of space, and the rise of the nuclear family have been expressed in house designs, which embody ideas about the household and gender within it. For example, in their overview of the history of gender in house design, the feminist collective Matrix explore how upper-middle-class Victorian houses in the UK embody a concern with privacy and the separation between the adult couple and their children and servants.

Using the 1864 prescriptive manual *The Gentleman's House* and their knowledge of the gender associations of spaces within the house, they map out the spaces associated with men and with women in an elite London town house plan, showing that elite women's spaces were on the first floor and more private, while elite men dominated the more public spaces on the ground floor (figure 4.5). Servants, both male and female, populate the basement and servant rooms on the first floor, while a female nanny is associated with the top floor nursery that also segregated children from the adult life of the house (figure 4.6).[7] In this context, what it is to be male or female in this house is interwoven with being an adult or child and being master/mistress or servant. Mapping these intersectional roles, we can see that gender roles extend into the service spaces — with women more associated with the kitchen and men with the carriage and horses — and that both the kinds of service men and women do and the rooms in which they are visible serving reinforce the elite gendering of spaces. For example, while a maid would clean all the more public spaces, a butler and footmen would be visible serving in masculine spaces such as the dining room. As lower status members of the household, servants lived either next to their workspaces or in marginal spaces within the house, but in rooms strictly separated by gender and rank. However, their status as servants is more important than their gender. We can also see this pattern in imperial China, where female servants would cross boundaries between inner female-gendered space and the outdoors, and in apartheid-era Johannesburg,

FIG. 4.6. (*facing page*) Spaces for servants within this nineteenth-century English row house are similarly gendered. Male servants (coded with dots) occupy the male bedroom, butler's bedroom and pantry, and wine cellar on the basement floor; the carriage house on the ground floor; and the coachman's room on the first floor. They also serve in the library, front hall, and dining room. Female servants (coded with crosshatch) occupy the kitchen and related rooms, laundry, and housekeeper's room in the basement, and the servants' rooms on the first floor; they serve primarily in the drawing rooms and the upstairs floors (not pictured). "Design for a Row of London Houses," Robert Kerr, *The Gentleman's House, or How to Plan English Residences* (London: John Murray, 1865), plate 44. Spaces coded by the author, indicating gender of servant residents.

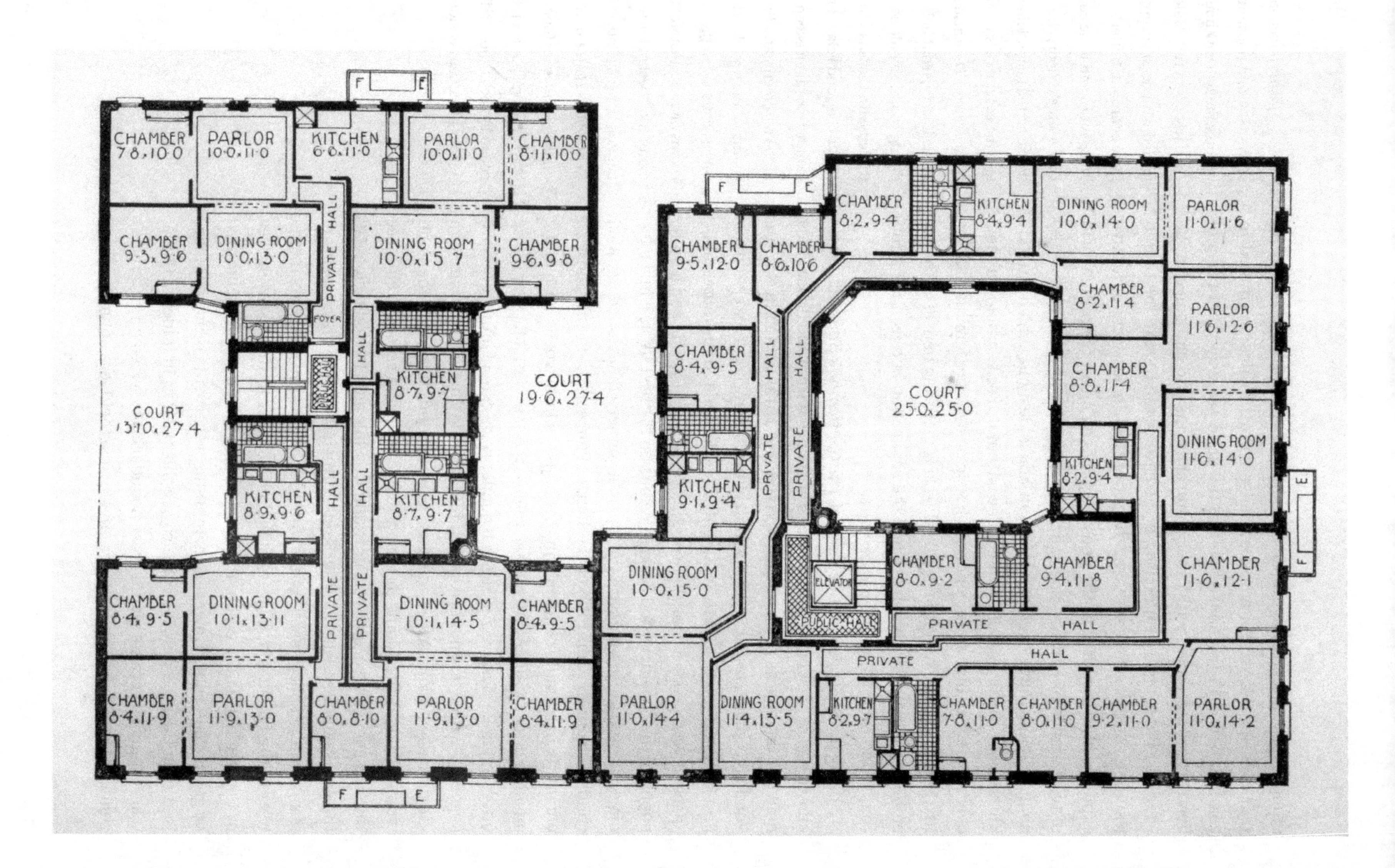

CHAMBER 7·8 x 10·0
PARLOR 10·0 x 11·0
KITCHEN 6·6 x 11·0
PARLOR 10·0 x 11·0
CHAMBER 8·11 x 10·0
CHAMBER 9·3 x 9·6
DINING ROOM 10·0 x 13·0
PRIVATE HALL
FOYER
DINING ROOM 10·0 x 15·7
CHAMBER 9·6 x 9·8
HALL
KITCHEN 8·7 x 9·7
COURT 13·10 x 27·4
COURT 19·6 x 27·4
PUBLIC HALL
KITCHEN 8·9 x 9·6
KITCHEN 8·7 x 9·7
PRIVATE HALL
PRIVATE HALL
CHAMBER 8·4 x 9·5
DINING ROOM 10·1 x 13·11
DINING ROOM 10·1 x 14·5
CHAMBER 8·4 x 9·5
CHAMBER 8·4 x 11·9
PARLOR 11·9 x 13·0
CHAMBER 8·0 x 8·10
PARLOR 11·9 x 13·0
CHAMBER 8·4 x 11·9
F E
CHAMBER 8·2 x 9·4
KITCHEN 8·4 x 9·4
DINING ROOM 10·0 x 14·0
PARLOR 11·0 x 11·6
CHAMBER 9·5 x 12·0
CHAMBER 8·6 x 10·6
CHAMBER 8·2 x 11·4
PARLOR 11·6 x 12·6
CHAMBER 8·4 x 9·5
PRIVATE HALL
PRIVATE HALL
COURT 25·0 x 25·0
CHAMBER 8·8 x 11·4
DINING ROOM 11·6 x 14·0
KITCHEN 9·1 x 9·4
KITCHEN 8·2 x 9·4
DINING ROOM 10·0 x 15·0
ELEVATOR
PUBLIC HALL
CHAMBER 8·0 x 9·2
CHAMBER 9·4 x 11·8
CHAMBER 11·6 x 12·1
PRIVATE HALL
PRIVATE HALL
PARLOR 11·0 x 14·4
DINING ROOM 11·4 x 13·5
KITCHEN 8·2 x 9·7
CHAMBER 7·8 x 11·0
CHAMBER 8·0 x 11·0
CHAMBER 9·2 x 11·0
PARLOR 11·0 x 14·2

where most Black servants, whether male or female, were housed in shanty-like "back houses" at the boundary of suburban lots.[8]

Twentieth-century servantless houses in the US and Europe often replaced the hidden labors of servants with the hidden labor of the housewife. Kitchens, washrooms, and pantries were hidden from the public spaces of parlors and dining rooms, even when the labor performed within them was done by a family member (figure 4.7). Houses for working-class families followed this middle-class model, as public housing was created not only to serve an underhoused population, but also as an attempt to teach them middle-class ways. The Frankfurt Kitchen, designed by architect Margarethe Schütte-Lihotzky in 1926 for model working-class housing and used broadly in Germany and the USSR, accommodated one person in a highly efficient space, turning the kitchen into a one-person factory (figure 4.8). The intent was to free women by making their work more efficient, as well as to elevate the work of the housewife by modernizing it. But in practice, because the kitchen only fit one person, it isolated the housewife spatially from the rest of the house and made the necessary simultaneous work of childminding difficult.[9] Similarly, the housing manual created by the UK Central Housing Advisory Committee in 1944 focused on ameliorating women's labor in the kitchen through technology and conceptualized a woman's role within the house as serving her husband and children.[10] These designs continued to express the idea that kitchen labor is something to be hidden, just as it was in earlier middle-class designs that hid servants and their work. In so doing, they functionally turned the woman of the house into a servant for the rest of the household.

Mid-century modern houses for a middle-class audience in North America similarly featured small kitchens and "laborsaving" technology but often made them more open to the rest of the house and more central within the plan. With an open counter or a pass-through that can be opened, mid-twentieth-century houses continued to cast the woman as the servant for the household but added in ways to supervise children (figure 4.9). In addition, rather than hiding the woman's kitchen labor, many of these houses made the figure of the woman visible, so that her body, as well as the kitchen, was the core around which the house was organized. The design of kitchens shifted to fit this change in visibility, with matching-colored appliances, decorative and colorful coordinated pots and pans, and attractive flooring. The centrality of

FIG. 4.7. (*facing page*) In the St. Cloud and the Fernwood, 1906–1907, apartment buildings on Prospect Avenue in the Bronx, none of the apartments have a designated maid's room. In each, however, the kitchen is a service space separated from the other rooms by a private hallway. Lorenz Weicher, architect. From *Apartment Houses of the Metropolis* (New York: G. C. Hesseloren, 1908). New York Public Library Digital Collections, https://digitalcollections.nypl.org/items/510d47db-9f36-a3d9-e040-e00a18064a99.

FIG. 4.8. The Frankfurt Kitchen, designed by Margarete Schütte-Lihotzky in 1926, borrowed from galleys on trains to create a highly efficient kitchen. It was designed for a single user, with specialized places for each ingredient and activity. The kitchen is very much a service space, closed to the rest of the house. Minneapolis Institute of Art, https://collections.artsmia.org/art/95937/frankfurt-kitchen-margarete-schuette-lihotzky.

the kitchen and the woman working in it is particularly prominent in the 1956 Women's Congress on Housing, for which the Federal Housing Administration created focus groups of housewives from around the country to learn about their housing desires. The participants saw the kitchen as "the most important room in the house both in function and location" and "the heart, the core, the center, the focal point, the pivotal point" of the house which needed visual continuity with children's play areas both indoors and out.[11] The conceptual plan that accompanied the report expresses this centrality, with all other rooms subservient to the kitchen (figure 4.10). While new technologies, pre-prepared food, and ready-to-cook groceries made the kitchen potentially less dirty,

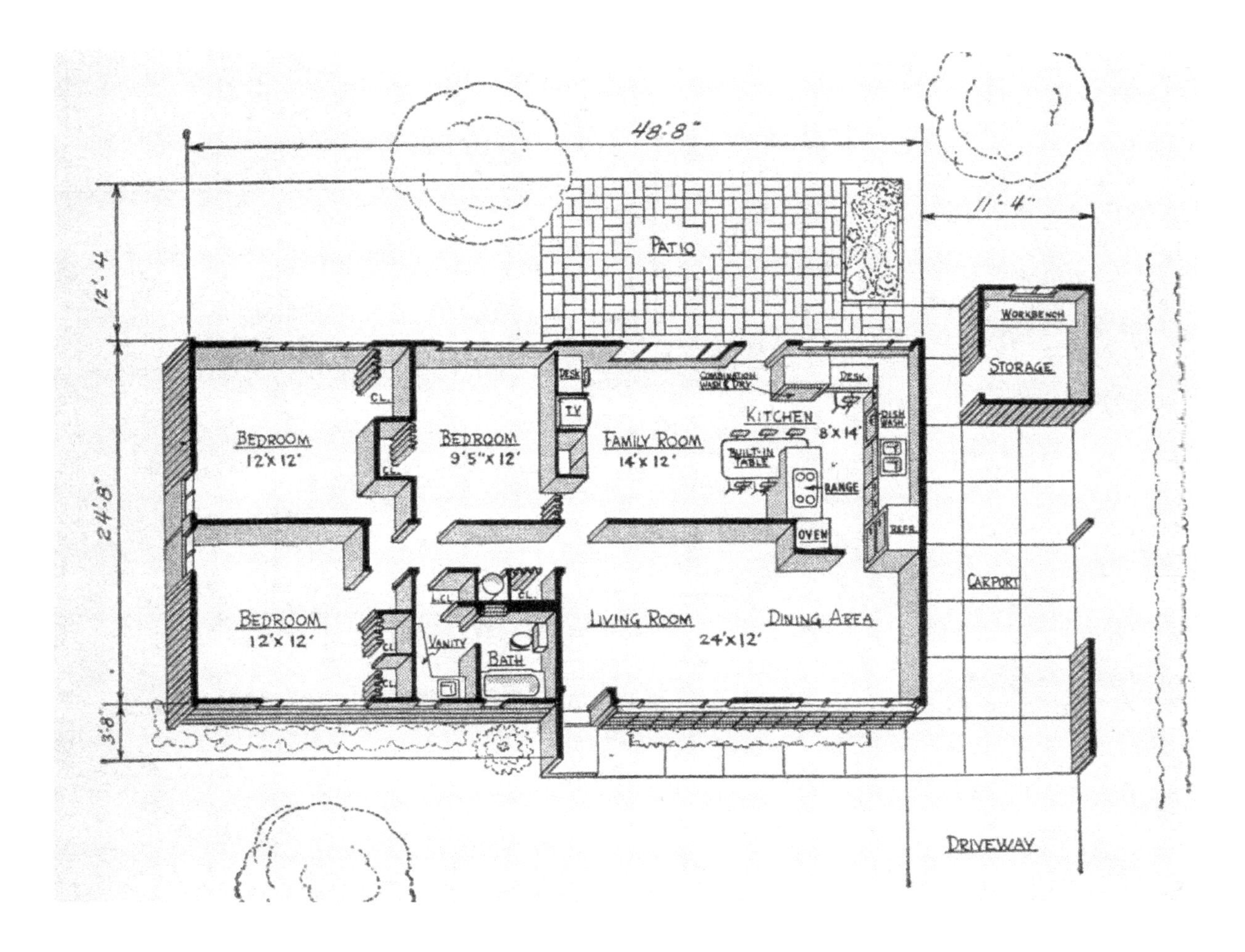

FIG. 4.9. This house in Jackson, Mississippi, by Edward J. Welty, architect, is a typical 1950s suburban plan. Rather than being separated from the rest of the house as a service space, the galley kitchen opens into the family room, with a table connecting them together. The mother is still serving the household from the one-person kitchen, but the plan ties together cooking and watching over children in the family room. *Household*, Nov. 1956, 26.

the open kitchen raised the expectation that it be ready to be seen at all times, removing any backstage space. As Dolores Hayden has argued, the rejection of any idea of collective cooking combined with the visibility of kitchens and kitchen labor increased the burden on women and tied them more fully to the home in a period of increasing separation between feminized suburban domestic space and masculinized urban landscapes of work.[12] The centrality of the kitchen ties in with the idea in this era that the house, and the suburbs within which it was located, was entirely the domain of the female head of household, who organized and decorated everything, such that men were chased to the backyard and garage to find masculine space. However, although the house might be feminized, prescriptive manuals and popular culture, including magazines, films, and TV shows, made it clear that the house did not exist for a woman's pleasure but rather as a tool through which she could serve her husband and children.

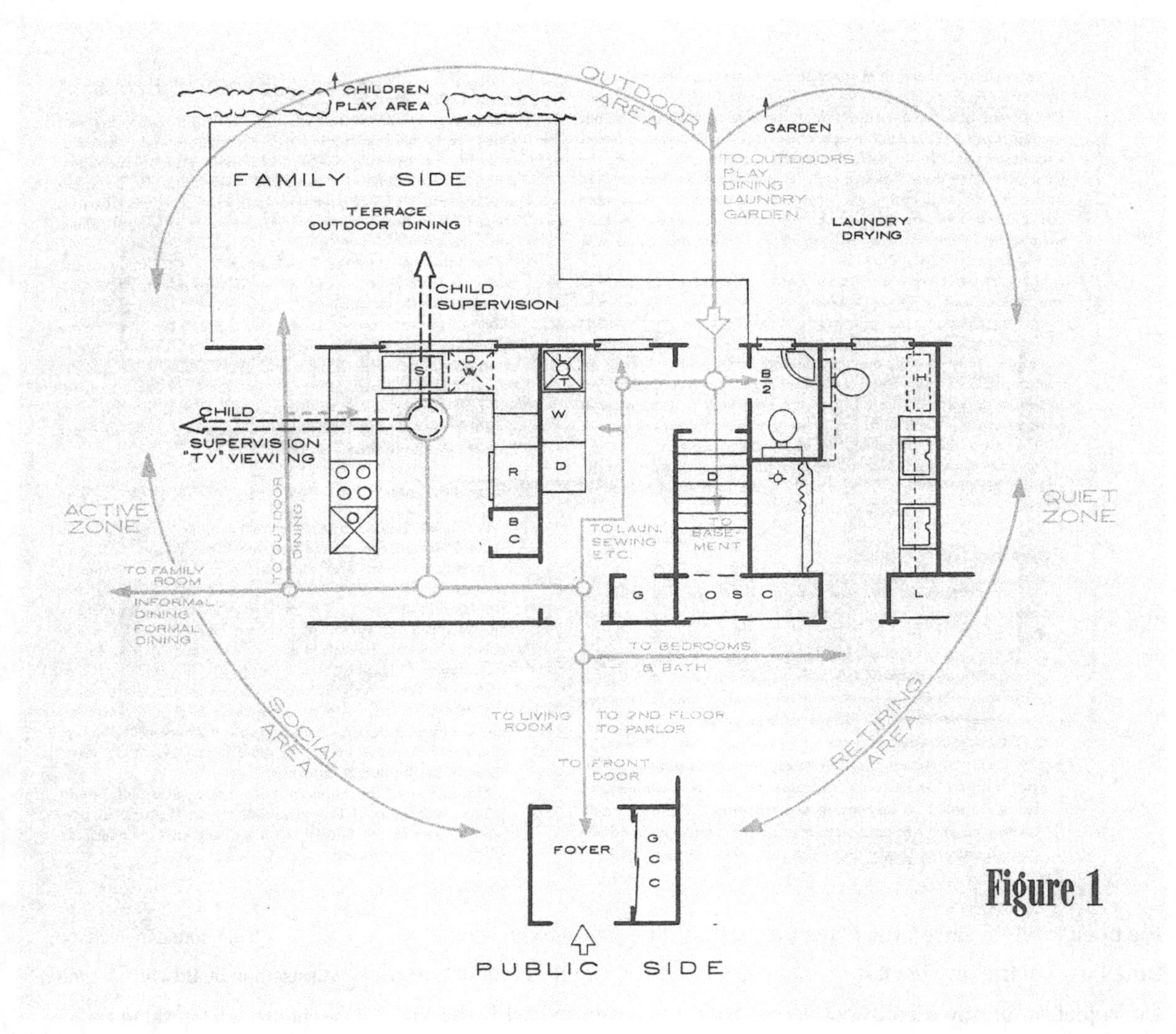

FIG. 4.10. This drawing expresses ideas about house layout coming out of the Women's Congress on Housing in 1956. The kitchen holds a central panoptic position, from which the mother can supervise children both in the backyard and the family room and also watch TV. Figure 2 from US Housing and Home Finance Agency, *Women's Congress on Housing*, 1956, 67.

GENDER AND HOUSE INTERIORS

Home spaces are typically marked as gendered through furnishings and interior treatments. For example, in the 1950s and 1960s, many kitchen appliances were available in pink and other pastel colors and, together with flower-sprigged pots and colorful paint, marked the kitchen as a definitively feminine space. Pastels, including pink, had an association both with the lightness of femininity and with children going back to the nineteenth century. But the gendering of pink in particular as a feminine color solidified in the twentieth century, and by the 1950s, it was increasingly present in interior finishes from refrigerators and radios to bedclothes, emphasizing the femininity of the home.[13]

FIG. 4.11. Parlor in Longfellow House, 1914. This fashionable parlor features light colors, a profusion of patterns, shiny upholstery, and numerous objets d'art. Light colors, shiny surfaces, and pattern have all been associated with femininity in design, contrasted with dark colors, matte or rough surfaces, and plain surfaces, which are associated with masculinity. National Park Service, LONG 27885.

Ninety years earlier, in the middle-class Victorian house, which had a plethora of specialized spaces, a clear design vocabulary emerged to signal the distinction between more female-gendered spaces such as the parlor and boudoir and masculine spaces such as libraries and dining rooms. Surveying Victorian architecture and design advice books, Juliet Kinchin found a broad set of principles anchored in the opposition between light and delicate feminine design and dark and heavy masculine design.[14] Physical lightness, expressed through color, shine, and lightweight and lacy materials, is tied to cultural lightness, to the idea that women are frivolous and lend joy to the household. Architect Hermann Muthesius, for example, wrote that the superficiality and lightness of social interchange in the drawing room "precludes seriousness in the decoration and content of the room."[15] Lightness was also symbolic of spiritual purity and hygiene, in contrast to the sooty and

FIG. 4.12. This mid-nineteenth-century sideboard belonged to the American businessman William T. Walters, who made his fortune in liquor and transportation. Like other high-style sideboards of this period, it is carved with dead animals, including fish, fowl, and mammals, celebrating both abundance and predation. High Sideboard with Hunting Trophies, American, c. 1855–1870. Walters Art Museum, accession number 65.132.

profane city. A light parlor then demonstrated that a woman had created an oasis from the city for her family, one which expressed spirituality (through, among other objects, parlor organs and religious-themed decorations), comfort, and refinement (figure 4.11).[16]

The masculine space of the dining room, in contrast, was a dark and serious space and embodied the role of the man of the house as breadwinner, most explicitly through hunting-themed paintings and sideboards elaborately carved with images of game (figure 4.12). Building on a close reading of mid-nineteenth-century sideboards, art historian and material culture scholar Kenneth Ames argues that the imagery of hunting and death celebrated not only masculinity broadly, but specifically White masculine predation, whether of animals, of colonized lands, or of business rivals in the dog-eat-dog world of nineteenth-

FIG. 4.13. This 1902 dining room in the William H. H. Pettus Residence in Missouri expresses masculinity through dark wood, both in the coffered siding and in the carved furniture, and through symbols of hunting, more subtly in the carved sideboard and very explicitly through trophy heads. The stag, often prominent in late nineteenth-century dining rooms, is an elite reference historically, as in Britain, only the aristocracy had the right to hunt deer. Photograph by White Studio, 1902. Missouri History Museum, Identifier N34248.

century capitalism.[17] Combined with leather and oak, the baronial imagery of hunting and dead animals marked the dining room as a masculine space, where the bounty brought home by the man of the house was enjoyed and men lingered afterwards to drink and smoke cigars while women retired to the parlor (figure 4.13).

Parlors and dining rooms are particularly interesting as gendered spaces because they were, of course, used by all members of the family and by guests, and thus it was not the gender of users that was expressed through interior design, but rather a set of gendered meanings that embodied the relationship between gendered roles within the culture and the social function of each room. Parlors serve as a space of entertainment and comfort, as well as a site for the performance of gentility, both through manners and through furnishings. In the nineteenth century in North America and the UK, it was women's role to civilize children and to entertain guests. The parlor was the space within and through which the women of the household expressed family status and did the labor of forging and maintaining social connections.[18] If the parlor expressed the woman's taste and her role as a consumer, the dining room expressed the man's role as provider and, along with more purely masculine haunts such as the den or library, contained the activities that tied men to each other, including indulging the noble vices of gluttony, alcohol, and tobacco.[19]

Elements of both the design language and the gendered meaning of rooms from the Victorian era have continued into the twentieth century and beyond. For example, in designs for bachelor pads in the 1950s and 1960s, a dark, textured, and clean-lined masculine design language with occasional references to the hunt was used to mark domestic spaces, including the usually feminine-gendered living room/parlor, as male. In *Playboy*, crepuscular illustrations show bare brick, fieldstone, leather, and wood in dark tones. In films such as *Pillow Talk* (1959) and *That Funny Feeling* (1965), dark leather, wood, and brick bachelor pads are contrasted with pastel and flower-bedecked women's apartments. The decorative impulse that is the signature of Victorian parlors is avoided assiduously; the description of Playboy's Penthouse Apartment focuses on that masculine absence: "lamps, which would impede the clean, open look of the place, are virtually dispensed with; there is a complete absence of bric-a-brac, patterned fabrics, pleats and ruffles."[20] Artworks are rare and modernist in bachelor pads, and the few examples of figurative art feature cave paintings of horses or prints of firearms, harkening back to the masculine hunting themes of the Victorian sideboard. The masculinity of bachelor pad designs is overdetermined because during this period the house and domesticity more broadly were gendered female; examining the popular culture depictions of bachelor pads in the context of the broader gender norms of the period allows us to interpret the bachelor pad as an expression of anxiety about men's autonomy in a moment of perceived masculinity crisis.[21]

Gender in Public Space

While houses express and enforce gender roles within the family and thus express heteronormative gender norms relatively explicitly, most nondomestic spaces are also used by a mixed-gender public and can be explored through a gendered lens. In many cultures, the distinction between domestic/private space and public space is gendered, and many feminists have argued that women's relegation to domestic space has been a major contributor to their oppression.[22] Public spaces, including workplaces, commercial spaces, and streets, are now used by both men and women in much, though not all, of the world. However, the gendered legacy of many of these spaces often lingers and affects how they are used and understood in the present. In some cases, the continuing effects of gender segregation in the job market mean that certain public and semipublic spaces remain dominated by a single gender. In others, collective memory and shared habits, including rules of etiquette and norms of policing, gender public space. A gendered legacy is also often expressed through gendered design language, which continues to communicate about appropriate users, even when the people using a space have changed.

WORKPLACES

Many jobs are highly segregated by gender, as well as marked by age, class, and race; thus, workplaces often function as gendered spaces even if they were not consciously designed as gendered. For example, 79% of elementary and middle-school teachers and 97% of preschool teachers are female, making schools, especially those serving younger children, a dominantly female-gendered space.[23] Similarly, only 2.3% of car mechanics are female, and garages are conspicuously masculine spaces, stereotypically marked through language, behavior, and girlie calendars.[24] But many workplaces are more mixed gender. Corporate offices are a fruitful place to examine the interrelationship of gender and the workplace, as they came into being as a specialized space in the late nineteenth century, a period of both heightened attention to gender and the remaking of downtowns into specialized commercial spaces of consumption, banking, and management. As businesses set up corporate offices in the late nineteenth century, they used principles of scientific management, sorting workers by task, fitting them into the minimal necessary space, and designing workspaces to maximize managers' ability to see workers at all times. While this organization of space is not explicitly gendered, jobs within offices were highly gender segregated, so the effect of sorting workers by task also sorted them by gender. Managers were also concerned about the dangers of the mixed-gender workplace both to women and to efficiency, and further separated workers by sometimes providing separate lunchrooms and

FIG. 4.14. In the mailroom of Southern Bell Telephone and Telegraph Company in the 1930s, the women sorting mail are shown being watched over by two male supervisors. There is no space for personalization on these tightly ordered desks. Photo by Royal Photo Company CC BY 2.5, https://creativecommons.org/licenses/by/2.5, Wikimedia Commons.

lounges for male and female workers (with parallel spaces for all-male executives) and by assigning different times for male and female workers to ride elevators and take lunch breaks.[25]

The desire to maximize managers' ability to see workers led to the creation of open rooms for lower-status workers, sometimes with a raised seat for a manager (figure 4.14). While both men and women were often grouped in these open rooms, the manager watching over them was typically male. Daphne Spain, in her exploration of gender, space, and status in the workplace, argues that the spatial organization of offices by role creates gendered spaces. Men, concentrated in upper management, have spaces with privacy and doors that close, while secretaries and administrative assistants, a job category that is still over 92% female, are in spaces with little privacy and which are usually shared with other workers.[26] Historically, typists often worked

FIG. 4.15. The organization of the twentieth-century typing pool expresses the interchangeability of women typists, who sit at identical desks in an open room. Head Office typists' room, New Zealand Railways, 1959. Archives New Zealand, https://www.flickr.com/photos/archivesnz/25557790294/in/photolist-EWsmCN.

in secretarial pools that could be called on for services by anyone of higher status. The space for secretarial pools was commonly an open room with multiple identical desks, a space with no privacy or space for personalization (figure 4.15). Technological transformations as well as changes in office design mean that the secretarial pool as such is no longer common, but the distinction between levels of privacy for managers and those in administrative support positions remains highly visible in office spaces. Managerial men's privacy is often guarded by highly visible women, including receptionists and executive secretaries.[27] High-level executive offices are often only entered through a reception room overseen by a secretary; one can easily recognize these offices on a plan because of this extra level of privacy (figure 4.16).

Office spaces have also been gendered through interior design. Executives have significantly more control over their spaces and often are provided a budget to decorate their office to their own taste. Early twentieth-century executive offices were decorated using elements of

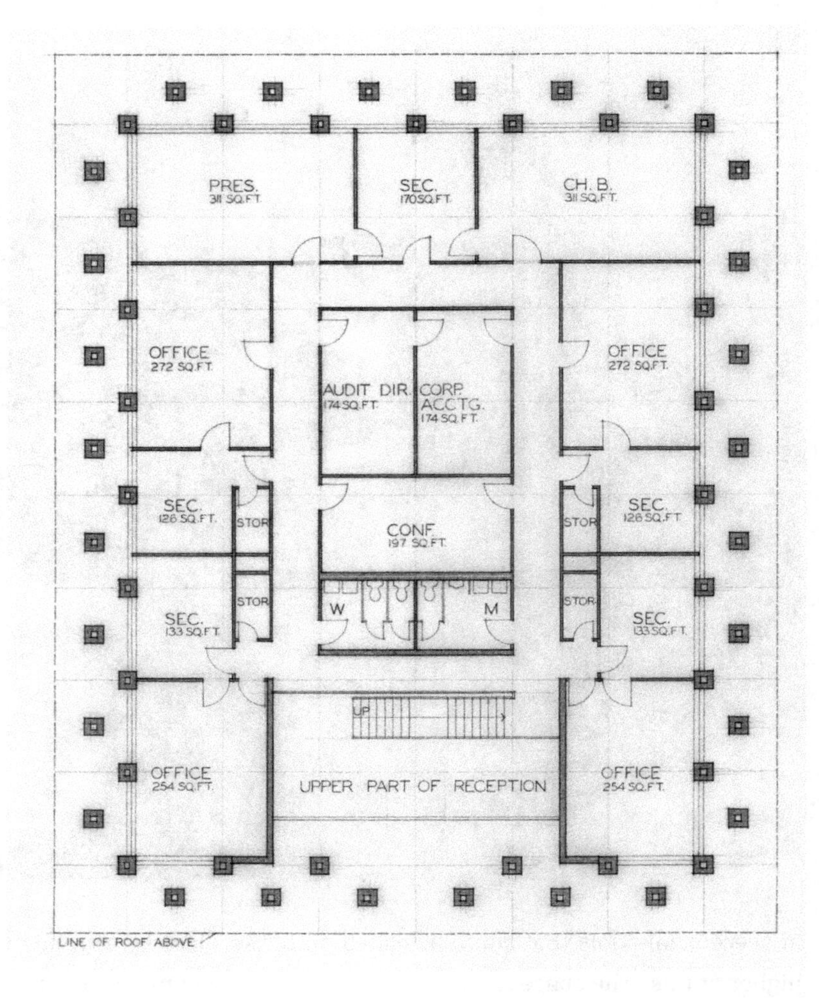

FIG. 4.16. In this 1966 corporate office, each executive office has an attached secretary's office, with a direct door between them. Plan for first floor of Westgate Research Park Corporate Headquarters, Old Springhouse Road, McLean, Virginia, 1966. Charles M. Goodman Associates, Architects — Land Planners, https://www.loc.gov/pictures/item/2022646155/.

masculine domestic design, including stone fireplaces, leather armchairs and couches, carpets, and animal-skin rugs, expressing richness and comfort (figure 4.17). Modernist offices in the mid-twentieth century similarly included elements that echoed contemporary living room and dining room furnishings. These domestic-style offices, Angel Kwolek-Folland argues, strengthened the imagery of corporate fatherhood and "validated the manhood of those who possessed them by emphasizing individuality and personal freedom," a power that was reinforced in some offices by attached private toilets.[28] In contrast, spaces for clerks and secretaries featured rows of identical desks, with no space for personalization and no echoes of the domestic realm. The shift to cubicles in the late 1960s and early 1970s democratized personalization, but the materials and forms of the cubicle, like the office desks

FIG. 4.17. The 1911 office of Charles Frohman, an American theatrical producer, uses elements from a domestic study, including the fireplace, skin rug, oriental carpets, and chandelier. This is a space of comfort, personalization, and luxury, a strong contrast to the spaces of lower-status workers. *Charles Frohman: Manager and Man* (New York: Harper & Brothers, 1916).

they replaced, are resolutely nondomestic, and their openness continues to contrast with the privacy of closed-door managerial offices.[29] More recent "hot desk" open offices continue this hierarchy, with most workers using varied spaces in the office, rather than an assigned desk, while upper executives still have private spaces. While office spaces explicitly reflect power differentials, rather than gender per se, the use of gendered design imagery and the relatively gender-segregated nature of the workforce mean that gender remains visible within them.

COMMERCIAL SPACES: RESTAURANTS

Commercial spaces like restaurants are designed for a particular clientele and reflect the gender ideologies of their users. Perhaps because they are places for the bodily pleasures of food and alcohol, restaurants have often been particularly expressive of gendered norms. In more gender-segregated eras, restaurants were often reserved primarily for men and were taboo for unescorted women. For example, eighteenth-century coffee shops in France and England were a purely male space, while most restaurants in the nineteenth-century US would not serve women unescorted.[30] The design of these spaces often used masculine design symbolism. For example, the restaurant Schroeder's in San Francisco, which would not serve women lunch until 1970, combined dark wood and leather with stag horns, beer steins, and a painting of a scantily clad woman riding a bottle of champagne. In

FIG. 4.18. The Chef's Place restaurant in Annville, Pennsylvania, signals its appropriateness for women through floral decoration, light colors, and family-sized tables. The family-friendliness is further underlined in the text on this advertising postcard, but the design itself telegraphs propriety. Postcard, 1920s.

FIG. 4.19. The Echo in Sandusky, Ohio, provides tables, but the space is dominated by the massive bar. Those drinking at the bar would need to stand, leaning on the railing. Numerous spittoons are provided for tobacco-chewing men to spit in, a sure sign of a space inappropriate for women. Postcard, c. 1907.

addition, private sheltered booths provided space for illicit activities. In turn-of-the-century hotels, men's grill rooms, dominated by large mahogany or stone bars, contrasted with light-colored ladies' dining rooms decorated with plants, providing gender-segregated spaces for elite diners.[31]

By the early twentieth century, mixed-gender restaurants, particularly family restaurants serving a working-class and lower-middle-class clientele, were increasingly common in the US.[32] Many family restaurants were run by immigrants to serve their compatriots, in locations on local main streets. Their interior design was quite different from masculine establishments serving the same class, with appro-

FIG. 4.20. The Boos Brothers Cafeteria in Los Angeles features small tables, white tablecloths, and lightweight bentwood chairs, signaling its appropriateness for women and families. The tiled wall and floor and gleaming cafeteria line at the back present an image of cleanliness and modernity. Postcard, c. 1910.

priateness for women signaled in part through small tables as well as through a lack of alcohol (figure 4.18).[33] In contrast, saloons and hash houses, the most common places for working-class men to eat out, usually had a bar or counter and only rarely tables (figure 4.19).[34] Even higher-status establishments serving men were often dominated by a bar, symbolizing the presence of alcohol. Some saloons had a separate ladies' dining room, tucked away from the main bar, often with a separate entrance, and furnished with tables. The sign "tables for ladies" commonly marked the presence of women within an assumedly male space. The tables provided women with some privacy, helping them to avoid being accosted by strangers. In addition, they made it possible for women to sit with decorum in a more comfortable, contained, and less visually powerful position than the men standing at a bar.[35]

In the early twentieth century, family restaurants were joined by the cafeteria, a new mixed-gender, mixed-class restaurant type. The cafeteria was defined by its self-service structure, in which patrons served themselves and carried food to a table of their choice, rather than being served at a table.[36] The design of the cafeteria reflected the norms of female-appropriate family restaurants but combined them with an image of modernity that reflected their novelty. They were typically decorated in light colors, and they nearly always provided seating in lightweight chairs at small tables (figure 4.20). Postcard images of cafeterias usually emphasize these tables, often covered with white tablecloths, even more than the novelty of the cafeteria line. The lightweight

FIG. 4.21. Automat, 977 Eighth Avenue, New York City, photograph by Berenice Abbott, 1936. In an automat, patrons serve themselves from coin-operated dispensers that are filled invisibly by workers on the other side of the wall. Even more than the cafeteria, the automat removes the supervising eye. From the New York Public Library, UUID 32d8d490-a7a9-013a-4b68-0242ac110003.

chairs were easy for women to move, and small tables provided privacy, a privacy enriched by the lack of table service. Other aspects of cafeteria design avoided previously gendered and classed design language through an image of modernity. The cafeteria system mimicked the modern assembly line, and the chrome, steel, and white enamel of the cafeteria line expressed its modernity. Cafeterias often used modern hard surfaces, such as white tile, which spoke of modernity and hygiene even as they subtly referenced feminine design norms.

The modernity of the cafeteria allowed it to function as a space that transcended classes; reading diaries of both upper-middle-class and poorer women, I found that they all mentioned eating in cafeterias. Often, the same cafeteria might serve a different clientele at different times of day. Depending on location, it might be frequented by blue-collar or white-collar workers, shoppers, or businessmen at lunch; families and young working people at dinner; and elite theatergoers or prostitutes and other disreputable diners late at night. Notably, all these populations, no matter their class, were mixed gender and could include women without male escorts. Cafeterias were an appropriate place for women to eat unescorted, especially since they did not serve liquor and did not use the design language of masculine eating places. The cafeteria also allowed a higher degree of privacy because of the lack of table service. The automat went even further, removing interactions with staff entirely, replacing them with the image of modern automation through food-serving machines (figure 4.21; see also figure 6.1). The comparative lack of policing in self-service restaurants also made them popular hangouts for queer men in the early twentieth century, a phenomenon I explore more in the next chapter.[37]

SIDEWALKS

Commercial spaces rarely sit on their own but are rather part of a broader cultural landscape epitomized by the main street and the shopping district. These specialized landscapes of shopping, entertainment, and dining out expanded significantly in the US in the mid-nineteenth century with the rise of consumer culture and the world of goods. The growth of commercial landscapes came about at the height of the ideology of separate spheres, in which public spaces and the world of business were gendered male and women were associated with domesticity and the home, which for the elite was located in increasingly specialized residential areas. In spite of this ideology, small-town main streets and portions of big-city downtowns served a mixed-gender public. The design and use of buildings and spaces within commercial landscapes helped to bridge the gap between the actual use of commercial landscapes and powerful cultural ideas about men and women and what spaces and behaviors were appropriate for them.

The buildings along main streets in mid-nineteenth-century small towns were specialized commercial blocks (figure 4.22). These were large buildings with elaborated façades and open storefronts with glass windows, often Italianate in style.[38] They were distinct from earlier main street buildings in their elaboration of the façade, their visual openness, and the separation of warehouse and retail space within them. These new buildings are often discussed in relationship to technological changes, such as innovations in glassmaking and the refocusing of iron industries from military purposes to cast-iron architectural

FIG. 4.22. This commercial building at 227 Meeting in Charleston, South Carolina, was built around 1840 and altered c. 1850. Like other commercial buildings of the era, it features a windowed ground floor shop that invites browsing and Italianate architectural features that signal attention to fashion. Upstairs rooms allow space for separate stockrooms. Historic American Buildings Survey, retrieved from the Library of Congress, https://www.loc.gov/item/sc0191.

elements. However, one of the prime drivers for these new buildings is new commercial activity which increasingly focused on women as shoppers. In her exploration of the main streets of small towns in Tennessee, Lisa Tolbert argues that merchants built or renovated shops with an eye to welcoming women shoppers into a space that comfortably and elegantly showed the wares for sale while hiding messier stock in basements and back rooms. Window displays behind plate glass provided an opportunity for merchants to attract female passersby into their shops, perhaps tempting them to buy. Using diaries and newspaper articles and noting the proximity of new women's colleges which attracted students from a broad geographical area to live near these main streets, Tolbert shows that women were regular denizens of small-town main streets in the mid-nineteenth century, and that the growth of small-town main streets was entwined with the mixed-gender nature of this commercial landscape.[39]

FIG. 4.23. View of Market Street from the Flood Building, 1915. Market Street served both shoppers and office workers as well as being the central spine of San Francisco's transportation, leading to a broad mixture of people on its sidewalks. In the foreground at the right is the Emporium Department Store, whose main entrance is through the large arch, while the entrance to the offices is through the smaller door to the left. *San Francisco Chamber of Commerce, San Francisco: the Financial, Commercial and Industrial Metropolis of the Pacific Coast* (San Francisco: H.S. Crocker, 1915), 78.

In larger US cities in the late nineteenth and early twentieth centuries, the downtown was imagined as made up of two separate cultural landscapes, a masculine office landscape and a feminine shopping landscape. Examining downtown San Francisco of this period, I discovered that in practice these two gendered landscapes had a significant overlap, especially along Market Street, which was the major transportation spine for the city as well as the location of San Francisco's first department store, the Emporium. While the shopping landscape was centered on department stores and associated smaller shops and services, including tea rooms and confectioners, it also included the wide downtown sidewalk, a space for leisurely strolling, where women could window shop, learning about current styles and offerings and marveling at elaborate displays. Examining the buildings that lined the sidewalk in areas that contained both shops and offices, I discovered a typical downtown commercial building type that segregated feminine shopping space, including the sidewalk in front of the store, and masculine office space (figure 4.23). On the ground floor these buildings housed shops with glass fronts opened to the sidewalk. Upstairs they provided several floors of offices, accessible by a more discreet entrance to the side of the shop or from another side of the building. The shops below and the offices above were fully separated from each other, such that one would have to exit to the sidewalk to move between them. These buildings expressed the ideal of gender separation by minimizing interaction between gendered interiors but simultaneously made the sidewalk a mixed-gender space, where windows and street speakers could address both men and women.[40]

Why Study Mixed-Gender Spaces?

Most spaces that we encounter in our everyday lives are mixed gender, including our homes, our workplaces, the places we go for fun, and the spaces in between. Because gender is a category that helps to structure society, it is present in mixed-gender spaces as well as in single-gender ones, although how strongly spaces are gendered varies significantly. In mixed-gender spaces we can more fully see the ways that gender functions as an axis of power. Architecture participates both in the gendering of spaces and in demonstrating power, through spaces such as kitchens, window offices, and open-plan workplaces. While the majority of spaces are mixed gender, only a small sampling of these spaces has been explicitly examined through the lens of gender. There are extensive opportunities to explore how gender and other intersecting axes of difference are expressed and shaped by public and domestic spaces throughout history.

The spaces that we have explored in this chapter are expressive of dominant gender structures, including the structure of heterosexuality. They express and enforce a gendered status quo that is centered on the heterosexual reproductive couple as well as on patriarchy, although in exploring how they change and how they have been challenged, they allow us to imagine future change in gender and in gendered architecture. In the next chapter, we will go beyond the expressions of normative gender embodied in both the single-gender and mixed-gender spaces we have examined so far by focusing on queer spaces, which challenge heteronormativity.

5

QUEER SPACES

Traditionally the built environment tends to be heteronormative, privileging dominant gender roles and identities. As we have seen in the previous chapters, the built environment both expresses and helps to shape binary ideals of gender based on the heterosexual couple and the reproductive family. Alternative models of gender, sexuality, and family are also visible within the vernacular built environment in spaces that have been shaped to fit the lives of queer and gender-nonconforming people. However, only rarely are spaces specifically built for a queer community. More often, spaces that were built with normative assumptions are used counter to those assumptions; they are "queered" through use. While a few buildings have been designed specifically to express and contain queer and gender-nonconforming lives, more are remade and remodeled, and many more are transformed through use and decoration. Spaces can be queered permanently, through design or collective memory; through long-term occupation; or through temporary, even fleeting, use, in which individuals function as "self-manifesting infrastructures of queerness, . . . bravely, or stupidly, changing the use and entire meaning of the spaces they [occupy], or [have] access to."[1] This chapter explores how to read vernacular architecture against the heterosexual grain, exploring some of the ways queer spaces, including apartments, bedrooms, bookstores, and bars, have been fashioned through both use and design.

Queerness and the Domestic Realm

As explored in chapter 4, homes express and shape ideas about the family and the gendered roles of family members. For many queer families and individuals, conventional housing can be a poor fit. Domestic spaces beyond the traditional house, including YMCAs and other single-room-occupancy hotels, have historically created a space for single men and women, including queer people searching for homosocial space. Some more privileged queer individuals and families have been able to create houses shaped to fit their particular idea of home, crafting alternatives to conventional houses for nuclear families. However, queer domestic space exists not merely in specialized spaces outside the traditional domestic realm, but also within ordinary houses and neighborhoods, where alternative uses of space, decoration, and even merely the presence of a nonnormative household can remake a conventional house as a queer realm.[2]

The convention of privacy for the family within the house has made it possible for interior spaces to be made over or constructed in ways that disturb heteronormative norms but remain hidden from prying eyes. Often, queer houses and households have found a home in towns or neighborhoods that already stretched conventional norms, whether bohemian, artistic neighborhoods like Greenwich Village or resort towns like Fire Island and Provincetown. Resort towns are heterotopic spaces, outside the everyday world of work, and provide a loosening of ordinary social rules as well as a place of retreat and privacy, particularly in the offseason.[3] Even within these towns and neighborhoods, queer households have often chosen exteriors that shelter their private space from public eyes, using strategies that vary from unassuming exteriors to blank walls. For example, Eleanor Raymond and Ethel Power's townhouse at 112 Charles Street in Boston, which they remodeled as a residence for themselves in 1923, presents a conventional façade to the world. Weston Havens's 1941 Berkeley house provides privacy by cascading down a secluded hillside site; it is barely visible to the street and was described by the architect as a "cave for moles."[4]

Behind respectable exteriors, the space within some queer homes breaks conventions to accommodate unconventional families. For example, the Scarab, a 1907 shingle-style house built for the Wellesley faculty couple Katharine Lee Bates and Katharine Coman, broke conven-

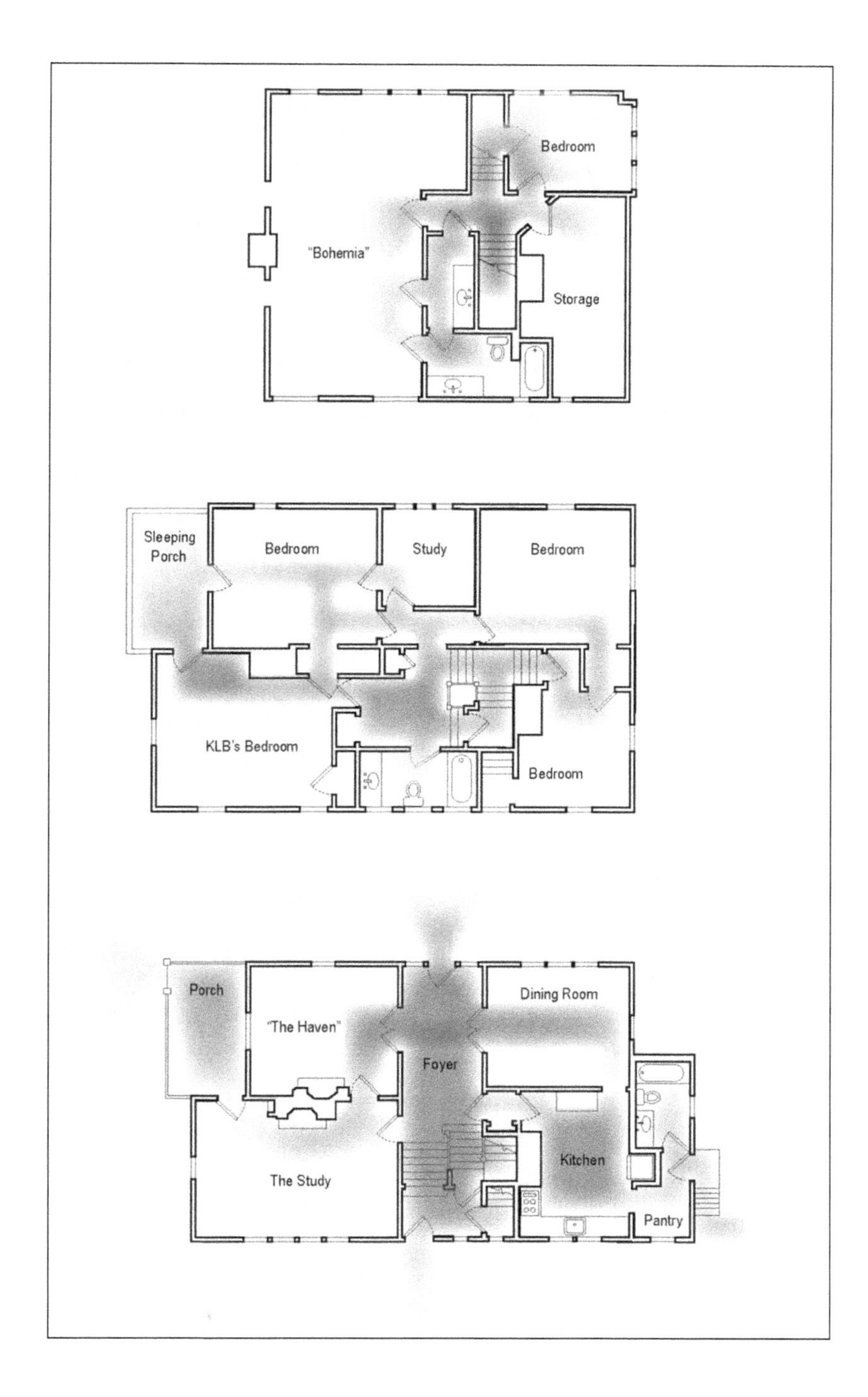

FIG. 5.1. The Scarab, the 1907 Wellesley, Massachusetts, home of Katherine Lee Bates and Katherine Coman, is unusual both in how it was used and how it was designed. The downstairs "Haven" and "Study" were used for writing and teaching, rather than functioning as front and back parlor, and students similarly took classes in the third floor "Bohemia." The bedrooms on the second floor flow from one to the next, connected through doors in closets as well as the central hall, defying the norms of privacy. Plan of the Scarab, Wellesley, MA, showing circulation. Drawing by Tabi Summers.

tions of private and public space in the home and housed not only Bates and Coman but also an ever-changing number of guests, students, and family members. In her analysis of the Scarab, Alice Friedman points out that the house is porous to the outdoors, with entrances not only to the front, but also from the garden into a large foyer that served as an

FIG. 5.2. The 1941 Weston Havens house in Berkeley, by Harwell Hamilton Harris, has three bedroom suites, each with a private bathroom (highlighted in this drawing). The upstairs suite overlooks an interior badminton court, while the ground-floor suites include terraces that open onto the court. The multiple equivalent bedrooms mark this as a queer and adult house, rejecting the hierarchical bedrooms of houses for nuclear families. Drawing by Tabi Summers.

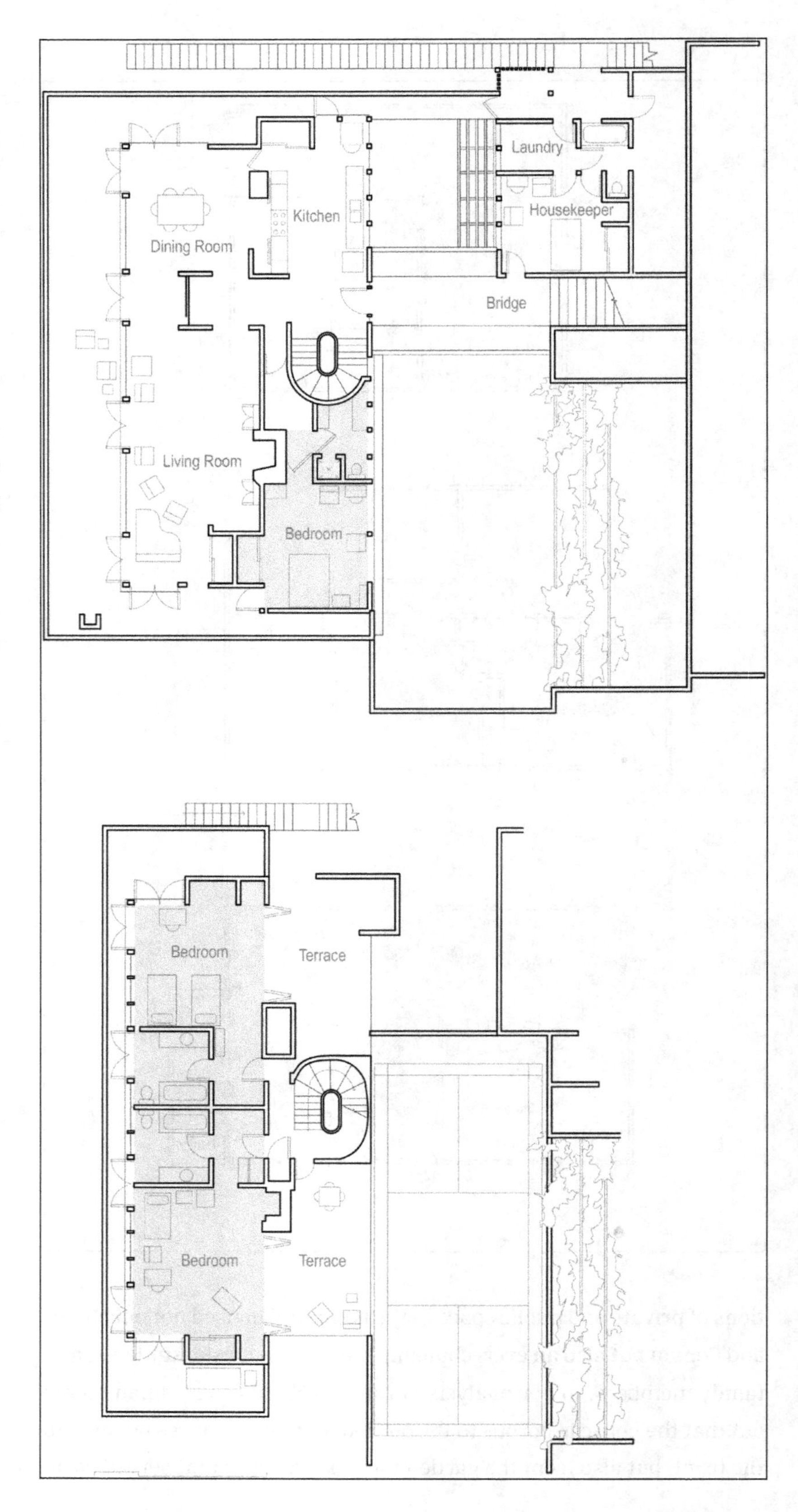

auxiliary living room and from a side porch into the front parlor (figure 5.1). The parlor, known as "the Study," was furnished with bookcases and a large mahogany desk and was used by Bates to teach seminars. Within the house, doors connect rooms directly to each other, most strikingly on the second floor, where the bedrooms are linked through large interior closets as well as accessible through a central hallway. Breaking the convention of public rooms on the first floor and private rooms above, the top floor held "Bohemia," Coman's workspace, where she wrote and taught classes. This house expressed the centrality of their professional identities, as well as the autonomy and equality of the two women, while creating a space for a broader female-only community that included relatives, students, and other guests.[5] Friedman uses archival evidence such as letters and memoirs to better understand the significance of the design of queer houses and to help discover which houses may reflect queer households.

Within homes, the organization of bedrooms is conventionally a major marker of familial hierarchy, with the "master bedroom," intended for the parental couple, noticeably larger and more advantageously located than other bedrooms, and typically provided with an en suite bathroom. Many queer houses, such as the Scarab, break this norm, with "multiple bedrooms that belong to no one in particular."[6] The Weston Havens House, for example, has three bedrooms of equal size, each with an en suite bathroom (figure 5.2). Like the multiple bedrooms in the Scarab, these bedrooms suggest not only a rejection of the hierarchies of the nuclear family, but also an expansive notion of the household, in which guests can partake of the safe private space of the queer haven in a context of intimacy that breaks down barriers between permanent and short-term residents. Many queer households have created family in ways that go well beyond the couple, tied together through affection, care, and community that can even expand beyond a single house.[7]

We can see a similar design of spaces that go beyond the nuclear family in resort towns. Houses in seaside resorts are often occupied by multiple unrelated people, whether a group of renters or owners and guests. Doubling up is common, so queer couples have often been able to rent hotel rooms or share rooms in rental houses without fear of exposure.[8] Many modernist houses in Fire Island, a longtime queer resort, feature multiple equivalent bedrooms that open onto decks that serve

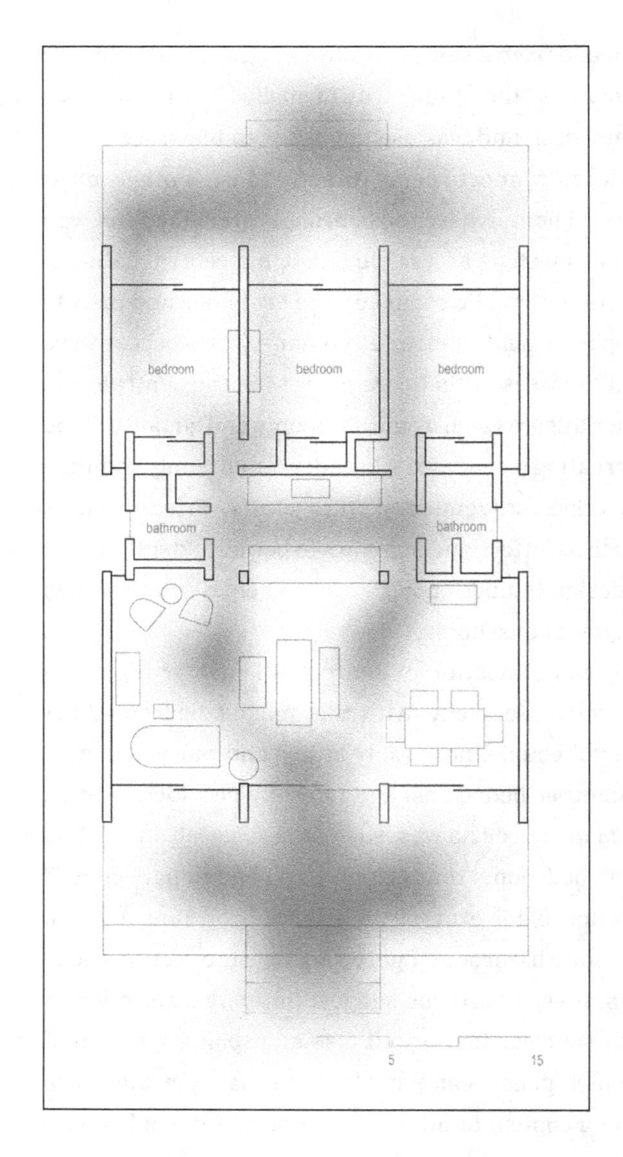

FIG. 5.3. The public rooms of the 1972 Angelo Donghia House on Fire Island, designed by Horace Gifford, open to a front deck, while the back of the house features three equivalent bedrooms, each opening onto a back deck. The bedrooms are strikingly nonhierarchical. Plan showing circulation drawn by Tabi Summers, based on *Architectural Digest*, Nov./Dec. 1973.

as places to sunbathe and rest, and also as the setting for parties (figure 5.3). Because resort towns exist for relaxation and pleasure, outside of the everyday, hedonistic architecture that houses multiple adults can easily become a norm.[9]

Many studies of queer domestic space highlight alternative modes of understanding public and private space within the home.[10] As a space of privacy, the house can provide a refuge from the heteronormative world; but at the same time, it often provides privacy and shelter not only for an individual or a couple, but rather for a community, especially in contexts where being their whole selves in public might not be or feel safe. Simultaneously, a queer house often functions as part of the public sphere, providing a space for political and social organizing and a safe space for queer parties, including rent parties and collective online parties during the COVID lockdown.[11]

While the Scarab and the Weston Havens House provide models of purpose-built queer houses, it is important to recognize that even the most conventional of houses can be analyzed as a queer space if we look beyond the ideology of the builders and designers and focus on users. Most LGBTQ households live in spaces that were not designed for them. Several scholars argue that a house is queered through the presence of a gay couple or individuals, and through egalitarian and nonheteronormative household practices, including domestic labor and childcare.[12] These practices are not necessarily visible architecturally, but they are an important piece of the history of a building and therefore key to comprehending its social and cultural meaning. Recognizing and examining queer use of domestic spaces can also help with understanding and mapping queer landscapes. Domestic spaces have historically been particularly important in lesbian cultural landscapes, which have often been centered on relationships between people and activities like softball games and picnics, which are ephemeral, rather than on gay bars and other visible queer public spaces.[13] Black queer communities similarly have often found community in rent parties and other house parties, in part because parties allowed them to escape the racism of White-dominant queer spaces.[14] Similarly, private suburban homes served as the primary space for social functions and smaller political meetings for the Detroit-area gay men of the Organization of Suburban People in the 1970s and 1980s.[15]

Kitchens in particular have served as spaces of political organization, workplaces for creating queer publications, and as the prime spaces of decision-making and discussion in collective households. The kitchen is a space for collective cooking and eating, acts symbolic of family. It has long been the site of lesbian potlucks, which have been at the center of lesbian community building and organizing since the Daughters of Bilitis began in 1955 as a lesbian social club that met mostly in members' homes over meals or coffee and pastries.[16] One older lesbian described the kitchen table as "a very grass-roots, self-made politics symbol," marked by a community of lesbians "sitting around and theorizing and fantasizing and making our own."[17] The importance of

FIG. 5.4. (*facing page*) In the 1920s, Max Ewing turned his closet into a so-called "Gallery of Extraordinary Portraits," expressing his sense of himself and his queer interracial world, both as experienced and as fantasized. Photograph, 1928, Max Ewing Collection. Yale Collection of American Literature, Beinecke Rare Book and Manuscript Library.

the symbol of the kitchen table and the space of the kitchen to lesbian identity and activism is visible in the naming of the pioneering Black-lesbian-founded Kitchen Table: Women of Color Press.

Decoration is a major way inhabitants make a house into a home, using objects which speak to their personal history, identity, taste, and personality, including photographs, books, and other objects.[18] Lesbians interviewed by geographers Lynda Johnston and Gill Valentine describe personalizing their homes through queer markers including images of lesbian icons such as k.d. lang and Martina Navratilova, lesbian books and music, and personal photos with lovers or lesbian groups.[19] This queer material culture served to make the home feel fully home-like and to enhance their identity as lesbians. Similarly, the residents of Transy House, a collective house in Brooklyn, decorated their individual rooms in pink and lilac satin and velvet fabrics, feathers, and flowers and marked them with sweet-smelling perfumes and candles to reinforce their sense of femininity. In shared spaces, trans power posters, a trans library, and shrines to Sylvia Rivera and Marsha P. Johnson, trans icons, are used by the residents to build a more political trans-positive collective identity.[20]

The material culture of interior decoration can speak to broad collective identities, through shared markers such as music, books, and queer icons, but it also is a means of constructing and expressing a unique individual identity. For example, in the 1920s, Max Ewing, a gay bohemian composer and writer, decorated a closet in his apartment with photographs and clippings of himself, friends, celebrities, and places he admired (figure 5.4). Alice Friedman, in her analysis of this closet, argues that it gives us a glimpse of his emotional life and the creation of one element in a queer, interracial archipelago in New York City.[21] Similarly, in his discussion of interviews with older LGBTQ people in the contemporary UK, Brent Pilkey focuses on the individuality of queer identities expressed through the decoration of entrance hallways, rejecting the idea of a shared queer aesthetic. For some of his interviewees, queerness is an explicit identity coded into their decorations; for example, Devin's hallway is filled with framed flyers from gay clubs he frequented when he was younger, many sexual and eroticizing the male body. Dean's is more symbolic of a queer identity, using images of opera divas and a collection of opera CDs to reference his identity as a queer diva. In contrast, Eric's identity as a gay man is only legible to

One side of Max Ewing's gallery of "Extraordinary Portraits" in his clothes closet.

FIG. 5.5. Rainbow flags like this one declare a queer presence in suburbia just as they do in cities, marking ordinary single-family houses as queer space. Suburban rainbow flag decoration, 2021. Photograph by Nicole Schroeer.

those who know his personal history, as his décor is made up of mementos of travels with his husband.[22]

Queer material culture also communicates identity to visitors, except when residents deliberately "de-dyke" or "straighten up" to hide their sexuality from more conservative family members or visitors. Material culture can also be used to publicly express queer identity, for example, by lesbians hosting office gatherings in their queerly decorated home, or by hanging a publicly visible rainbow flag.[23] In postwar and later suburban landscapes, while the house and backyard are resolutely private, the front yard and the front façade serve as the space to communicate through symbols of identity, including team banners, signs celebrating high school seniors, political signs, and rainbow flags — symbols of the ubiquity of queer suburbanites in the context of a broader cultural imaginary that equates queerness and urbanity (figure 5.5).[24]

In exploring queer domestic spaces, it is also important to include domestic spaces beyond the single-family home or apartment. Single-room-occupancy apartments and hotels have long provided spaces for

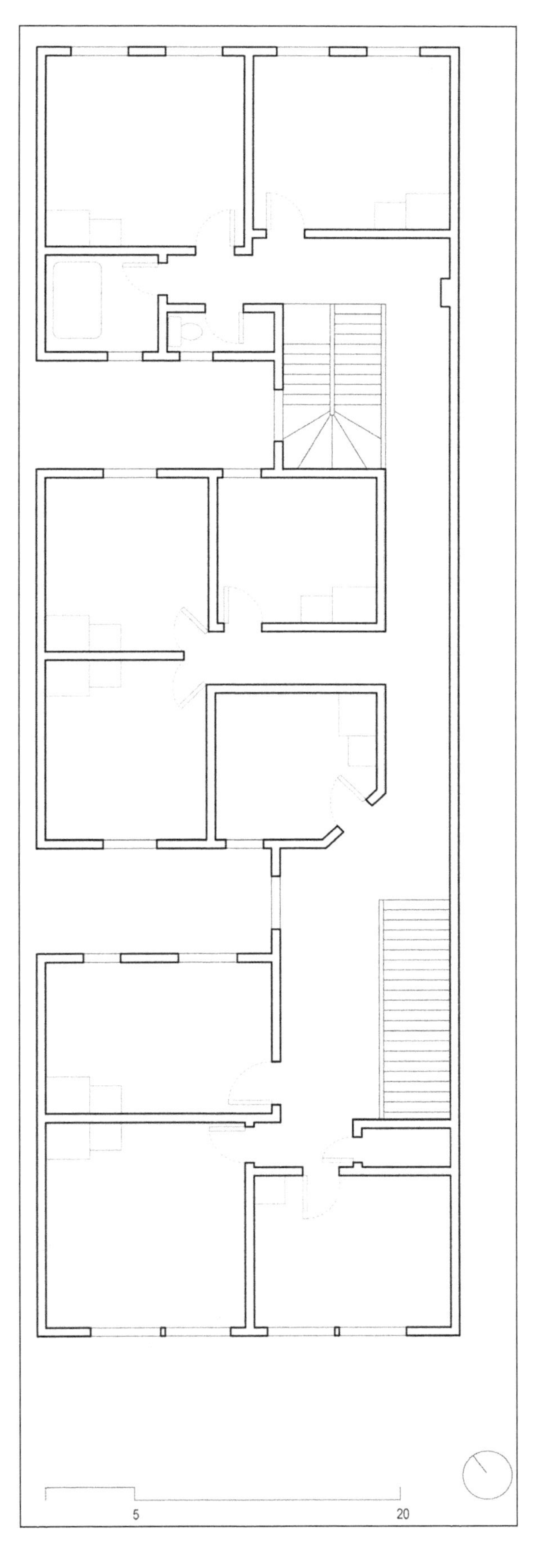

FIG. 5.6. In the 1910 Delta Hotel in San Francisco, the occupants of nine rooms all share a single toilet and bathroom, blurring the lines of privacy. Floor plan drawn by Tabi Summer, from Paul Groth, *Living Downtown: The History of Residential Hotels in the United States* (Berkeley: University of California Press, 1994), 98.

single people outside the structure of the nuclear household. As Paul Groth explores in *Living Downtown*, middle-class social reformers objected to housing that catered to single people because of its contrast to the heteronormative single family. They argued that hotel living made it too easy for young people not to start families and that the different lines of public and private in hotels led to moral laxity.[25] While residents in hotels and rooming houses usually had private rooms, they often shared bathrooms with unrelated people and ate and entertained either in hotel dining rooms and parlors, in more elite hotels, or in commercial establishments, all highly public spaces in comparison to private dining rooms and parlors (figure 5.6). This housing designed for people outside the nuclear family was attractive to many queer individuals, who found community with other residents. Using interviews, diaries, letters, police reports, and other sources, George Chauncey describes a gay male world in early twentieth-century New York that extended from YMCAs and rooming houses to more expensive bachelor flats where middle-class men could live in an all-male world. Individual rooms or flats allowed men a level of privacy they did not enjoy when living with a family, and the comparative lack of surveillance in hotels created a safe space where gay men met each other and were introduced to a larger gay social world. Ironically, a focus on heterosexual impropriety kept the focus off same-sex couples, who found queer community in single-sex institutions such as the YMCA. The YMCA hotels' gyms, swimming pools (where men swam naked), parlors, and dining rooms functioned as centers of gay male life frequented even by New Yorkers who gave fake addresses so that they could stay there on the weekends.[26]

The opportunity to create queer community in single-room-occupancy hotels has led to them sometimes being transformed into a home for an alternative queer community. For example, the trans women who lived in the El Rosa Hotel in San Francisco's Tenderloin neighborhood in the 1960s described themselves as a family, with Amanda St. Jaymes, who managed the hotel, as the mother.[27] In Buenos Aires, Argentina, the Hotel Condolín was taken over by its trans women occupants in 1999 and turned into a cooperative in which the older members take on the familial titles of aunt and grandmother. Individual rooms provide privacy and a space for smaller gatherings, while a terrace and a larger ground floor space hosts parties, meals, and gatherings that tie the community together.[28] In interpreting single-room-occupancy hotels, it is important to recognize that in their contrast to the nuclear family, they should be understood not only in the context of young men and women moving to cities in search of waged work, but also in a history of queer community.

Public Spaces of Queer Community

Explorations of queer space architecture have often focused on gay bars and other queer gathering spaces. In these public spaces, collective queer identity is constructed and expressed; they are of particular importance to those looking for community and to those who do not have the freedom to express their identity in their domestic space. George Chauncey has argued that for many gay men at the turn of the century, privacy could only be had in public.[29] This public includes explicitly queer space such as gay bars, lesbian coffeehouses, gay bathhouses, and queer bookstores; places such as cafeterias that become important to a queer world, often because of a policy of tolerance; and other ephemerally queer spaces such as gay nights in clubs, the streets during the pride festival, softball fields, and public restrooms.

GAY BARS AND OTHER EXPLICITLY QUEER SPACES

Gay bars are the spaces most often discussed as exemplary of queer space, although they have historically been accessible primarily to White men.[30] As a clearly queer space, gay bars have provided a place for White men to find other queer men without fear of harassment and as a place to affirm their identity and learn the culture of queerness. As Jeremy Atherton Lin writes in *Gay Bars: Why We Went Out*, "we go out to be gay."[31] The physical structure of the bars themselves as well as how they were peopled are expressive of what "being gay" has consisted of culturally in different historical periods and in different cultural contexts.

While bars and restaurants with a significant queer clientele have a long history, it is not until the 1960s that we see explicitly gay bars, providing a specifically queer space to drink and dance. Before then, most bars had a mixed clientele, and were often queer only at certain hours or on certain nights, meaning that the danger of violence or arrest was always present.[32] In addition, laws against cross-dressing and against people of the same sex dancing together enforced a politics of

FIG. 5.7. The Loading Dock bar in the South of Market District in San Francisco is located on an upper floor on a street of car-related businesses, above an auto-glass repair shop and next to a tire shop. Like many gay bars, the Loading Dock is in an area without many residents or other nighttime activity, making it less likely to be challenged by neighbors. Drawing by Jessica Sewell, based on c. 2010 photograph by Bob Meyers, http://www.bobmeyers.com/gay_san_francisco_soma.htm.

respectability in many establishments with a queer clientele. With the expansion of gay bars in the 1960s–1980s in the context of changing regulations and the growth of the gay rights movement, bars often reflected the idea of the closet and expressed the fear of being outed or arrested. The closet refers to the idea of hiding gay identity, particularly in a context in which to be out could endanger jobs, safety, and relationships with family, and is a term and an idea that began to be articulated in the 1960s.[33] Several scholars have explored the metaphor of the closet in relationship to architecture, exploring how private spaces, including Philip Johnson's bunkerlike bedroom pavilion and playboy Brad's hidden bedroom in *Pillow Talk,* served to conceal and disclose queer sexuality.[34]

The ways that gay bars served as closets, places to conceal their denizens from public view while disclosing themselves to each other, are visible in bars' locations as well as their designs. Bars founded in this period were often located in marginal and industrial spaces including waterfronts, skid rows, and areas next to highways and railroads. For example, many early gay and leather bars in San Francisco were located in the South of Market district, home to warehouses, light industry, and a working-class and transient population, often living in single-room-occupancy hotels. When Barbara A. Weightman surveyed 60 gay bars across the US from 1977 to 1979, she found that two thirds of them were located in what she called "zones of discard," and the remainder were on commercial strips near car lots, building supply stores, and the like (figure 5.7). These marginal locations, she argues, are zones of tolerance, where neighbors are unlikely to complain, as well as spaces where bar patrons are unlikely to encounter acquaintances from the straight world.[35]

Questions of public and private are central in the architecture of gay bars. The bar itself is a public space, a space of collective identity in which individuals, Jeremy Atherton Lin argues, are often abstracted into bodies and anonymous types, part of a crowd of gay masculinity.[36] But the gay bar is also a refuge, a place away from the heteronormativity of work and (often) home, where everyone is assumed to be queer, leaving behind the exhausting work of either maintaining the closet or repeatedly coming out. As Joan Nestle, cofounder of the Lesbian Herstory Archives, writes of a New York lesbian bar, the Sea Colony, "we needed the lesbian air of the Sea Colony to breathe a life we could not anywhere else. . . . Here and in other bars like this we found each other and the space to be a sexually powerful butch-fem community."[37] The shelter of the space of the gay or lesbian bar, its privacy from the straight world outside, created space for the creation of a collective public.

Gay bars from the era of the closet express a separation from the public realm of the street, they are "dark spaces with discreet entrances and exteriors," sometimes with entrances hidden down a back alley.[38] Windows filled in with glass brick, painted black, or blocked with paper, curtains, or one-way mirrors serve to keep the interior secret from the street, such that the bar functions as a public closet, a place apart from the everyday world outside (figure 5.8). While shielding the interior from the street was ubiquitous in the 1960s–1980s (about 90% of the bars Weightman surveyed in the late 70s had no view inside), it is still a common design feature, particularly in bars located away from populous urban gay neighborhoods. Not only are closeted gay bars disconnected visually from the street, but they also have other layers of defense between the protected space within and the mixed space outside. Anterooms and partitions, often marked with signs indicative of the desired clientele and sometimes guarded over by a bouncer, both shield the bar from the street and deter inappropriate patrons (figure 5.9). Sometimes a staircase adds another layer of buffering between the bar proper and the street. Inside the bar, the ability of the bartender to see everything was paramount, and bartenders used this surveillance

FIG. 5.8. At the Silverado in Portland, Oregon, mirrored windows hide the interior of the bar from the street. Photograph, 2013, by Another Believer, CC BY-SA 3.0, https://creativecommons.org/licenses/by-sa/3.0, Wikimedia Commons.

to police bars both to guard against behavior that might endanger their liquor license and to protect patrons from violence and police.[39] Lesbian bars as well as gay men's bars were hidden from the street and surveilled. Nestle remembers how in the 1950s, to protect both their patrons and themselves, managers of lesbian bars would flash a red light before the police arrived, so that patrons dancing (in an area well hidden from the street) would sit down and thus avoid being arrested for same-sex dancing. While this surveillance could be protective, it was also repressive, for example, controlling the bathroom so that only one person could enter at a time.[40] A mob presence further enhanced the sense of being controlled in lesbian bars, an experience Nestle describes

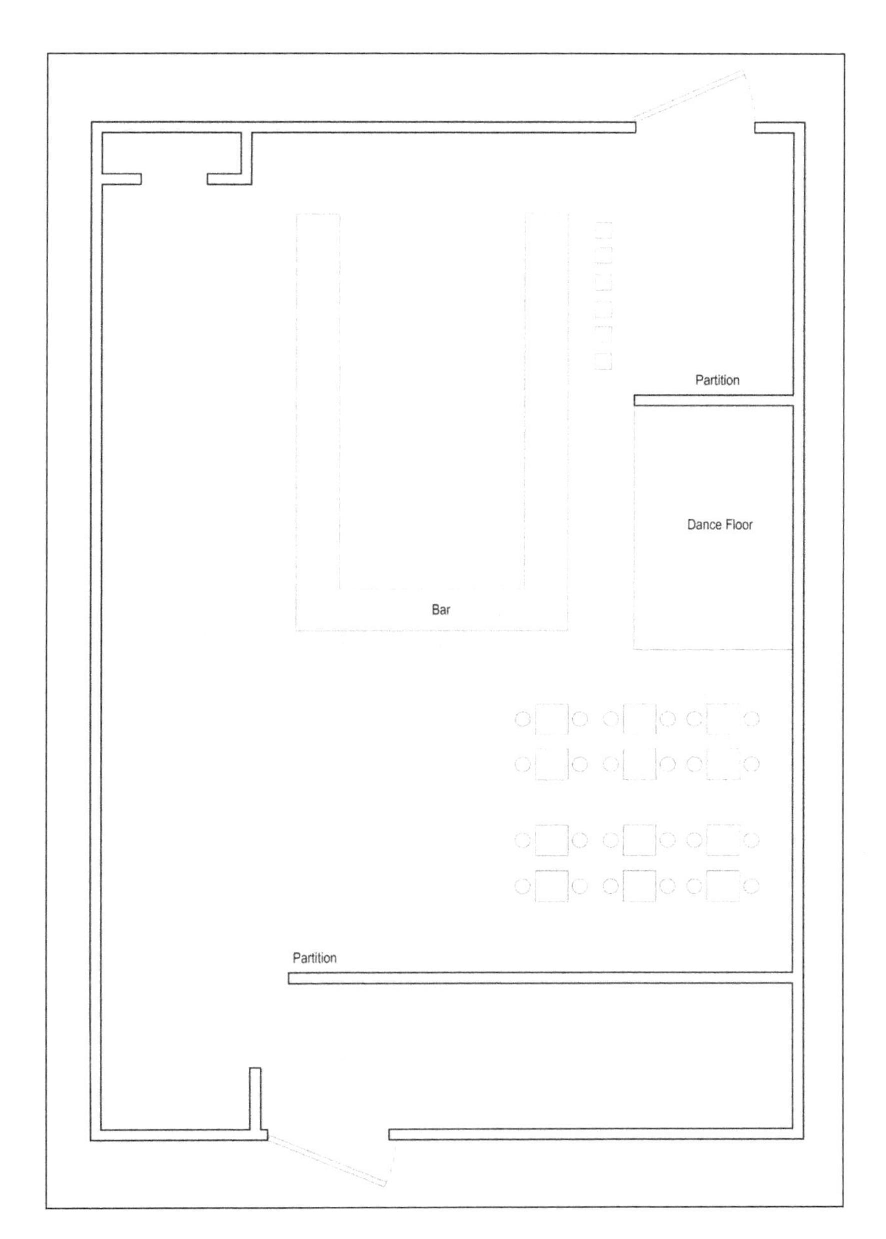

FIG. 5.9. In this plan of a typical gay male bar c. 1980, the interior is not visible from the front door, and entrants can easily be screened in the anteroom before they have access to the main space. A back door provides an escape from police raids. The central bar allows the bartender panoptic surveillance of patrons. Drawn by Tabi Summers, from Barbara A. Weightman, "Gay Bars as Private Places," *Places* 24, no. 1 (1980): 14.

as being "surrounded by the nets of the society that hated us yet wanted our money. Mafia nets, clean-up-New-York nets, vice-squad nets."[41]

In the early 1990s, a new style of gay bar which rejected the image of the closet opened in a few gay neighborhoods, including Soho in London, the Castro in San Francisco, and the Gay Village in Montreal. In contrast with the dark, enclosed façades of older bars, these new bars had open glass façades and spotless, stylish designs (figure 5.10). Jeremy Atherton Lin sees these new bars as a direct response to AIDS,

FIG. 5.10. The interiors of these twenty-first-century bars on Church Street in Toronto are visible to, and open to, the street, in contrast with the closeted bars of the 1970s and of many smaller cities and towns. Photograph, 2009, Neal Jennings from Toronto, ON, Canada, CC BY-SA 2.0, Wikimedia Commons.

communicating health and cleanliness, as well as associating gayness with upper-middle-class consumption.[42] The Complexe Bourbon, an elaborate bar complex in Montreal's Gay Village, epitomizes the contradictory effects of the politics of visibility. The Complexe Bourbon, begun in the early 1990s, clusters multiple gay bars and restaurants in one purpose-built corner building that features terraces that open to the street, blurring lines between inside and outside and emphasizing queerness as spectacle. Olivier Vallerand argues that the Complexe Bourbon functions as a flagship for gay tourism and an expression of a narrow vision of (White, male, rich) acceptable queerness, simultaneously celebrating gay presence while pushing aspects of queer community further underground.[43]

There is no single form for gay bars; they are expressive of local culture, the moment when they were created, the nature of their clientele, and much more. They range in size from New Sazae, in Tokyo, a gay disco the size of a small Tokyo apartment, to the over 10,000 square

FIG. 5.11. Bluestockings in New York City, like other feminist bookstores, provides a space for feminist and queer community. In 2021 it was turned into a cooperative, queer, trans, and sex-worker run bookstore and activist space. Photograph, 2006, by Alexa, CC BY 2.0, https://creativecommons.org/licenses/by/2.0, Wikimedia Commons.

feet of the Theatron in Bogota, Columbia, which combines a dance space in a former theater; a rooftop terrace that mimics the street, creating a simulacrum of safety in public; and multiple other spaces, all patrolled to repel any would-be queer bashers.[44] While there is no single architectural type for gay bars, we can gain insight into the significance of the space of gay bars by understanding them as part of a long history, recognizing the ways they have functioned as places of relative safety that affirm queer identities and spark queer joy. Interviews, oral histories, and participant observation will allow researchers to understand how the details of decoration, materials, and spatial organization function together to create specific experiences of queer identity.

Other permanent public spaces that have supported queer community include self-help, health, and community centers; queer and feminist bookstores; lesbian restaurants; and other queer-focused businesses. Many of these spaces have been shared; for example, feminist bookstores carry lesbian books but typically also serve a straight feminist population, while queer bookstores serve both lesbians and gay men. Many of the feminist bookstores that were founded across the US and Canada in the 1970s were founded by lesbians. They have functioned as resource centers, not only selling, recommending, and supporting feminist books, but also serving as community centers with information about a broad range of resources and as feminist spaces for a wide range of gatherings, from readings to consciousness-raising groups (figure 5.11).[45] The design of feminist bookstores reflects this community orientation. Oakland's Information Center Incorporate (ICI): A Women's Place, the first feminist bookstore in the US, was described by its members as different from other bookstores because "it has tables and chairs to sit and relax at, and coffee and tea and nibbles," and was "a pretty good size, so we can have rap groups, poetry readings, movies, etc."[46] Similarly, Pride and Prejudice in Chicago served free coffee to all comers, provided stuffed chairs and couches for reading or even spending the night in a pinch, provided space for all sorts of support groups, and housed a screen-printing workshop to make political posters.[47] Smaller stores sometimes make use of bookshelves on wheels to make space for events, including readings and receptions to celebrate feminist and queer writing and feminist political gatherings, such as a talk by members of the feminist dissident band Pussy Riot at Bluestockings in New York City in 2013.[48]

EPHEMERAL QUEER PUBLIC SPACE

Many queer spaces are temporary or ephemeral, ranging from regular gay nights at bars and weekly or monthly feminist coffeehouses in church basements, to the temporary occupation of a hotel for the length of a queer conference, to a space that is momentarily queered.[49] Any space can be queered depending on how it is used and by whom, but certain places are more easily open to recoding. Exploring queerness beyond the tightly defined space of a bar or a home allows us to see both what kinds of spaces open themselves to alternate genderings and how temporary queerings manifest spatially.

Spaces like function halls, church basement rooms, and conference centers provide an opportunity for queering because of their deliberate neutrality. Beige or landlord white, conventionally decorated if at all, they can easily be remade by the presence of visibly queer people, perhaps assisted by rainbow bunting. As spaces designed to be rented out to anyone, they are accessible to anyone who can afford them. Similarly, the generic public spaces of softball fields have provided space for the claiming of public lesbian identity and for lesbian sociability; in the 1950s and 1960s, one older lesbian told Anne Enke, "When you're new in town, the first thing you do is you look for the softball teams, because that's where you know you can find the lesbians."[50]

A gender-neutral design, tolerance of a broad clientele, and a lack of policing of behavior made cafeterias a prime space for queer community from their beginnings. Because cafeterias were self-serve, they were only lightly supervised by wait staff. At automats in particular, service staff were particularly scarce. Particularly late at night and especially in neighborhoods with a significant queer or bohemian population, cafeterias functioned as gay hangouts. In some neighborhoods, a gay presence, like the presence of artists, even served as a tourist attraction for cafeteria owners. The Life Cafeteria (previously Stewart's Cafeteria) on Christopher Street in New York was openly discussed in 1930s tourist resources as a "fairy hangout" and "one of the few obviously Bohemian spots left in the village," where "the more conventional occupy tables in one section of the room and watch the 'show' of the eccentrics on the other side."[51] The plate glass windows of cafeterias made the show of made-up men and other visibly queer people visible from the street as well as nearby tables, providing an opportunity for open performance, one sometimes made use of by tourists who gawked from the street.[52] It is not accidental that the first gay rights uprising in the US, San Francisco's Compton's Cafeteria Riot of 1966, began as a response to police harassment of transexual women in a Tenderloin cafeteria.[53]

Why Study Queer Spaces?

Focusing on queer space opens our eyes to the richness of how spaces are used in ways that resist the cultural norms that initially shaped them. Studying queer spaces helps us understand that the physical building is only one element of vernacular architecture and cultural landscapes; often what is most significant about a particular building is how it has been used and the meanings it has taken on, rather than its materiality. Studying queer space can also open our eyes to all kinds of daily practices that contradict built assumptions, whether using a lodge hall for a punk concert, transforming an apartment designed for a family into a space for unrelated roommates, or turning a garage into an apartment, music studio, or office. Studies of queer space can serve as a model for thinking more broadly about how users create meaning. Queer spaces can help open our eyes to the creativity of everyday life and the multiple possible meanings and uses of a vernacular building.

Ideally, studies of queer space allow us to understand how the meanings of spaces are layered and complex, not singular. YMCAs for example have simultaneously been spaces created by elites to shape virtuous young workers; sites of racial and ethnic inclusion and exclusion aimed at the Americanization of immigrants; housing for impoverished young men finding their way in the city; and centers of gay male community, for long-term residents, newcomers, and closeted men who take a vacation from their everyday married life to spend a gay weekend at the Y. Within studies of queer vernacular architecture as well as in vernacular architecture studies more generally, scholars often ignore elements of this complexity, not addressing, for example, the extent to which gay bars and dance clubs have served primarily White men. Lesbian public and collective spaces have been explored largely by historians and geographers and are ripe for analysis from a built environment point of view.[54]

It is equally important to study queer space because queer people are a part of all cultures, although queerness has been understood and experienced in culturally and historically specific ways in different places and times.[55] We study vernacular architecture in large part because it expresses culture; it tells us about how people have lived and what matters to them. To ignore queer spaces would be to tell a partial story, one that prioritizes the more powerful. Vernacular architecture study came into being out of a desire to go beyond the canon of architectural history and create a more inclusive history that includes the poor, the illiterate, immigrants, and minoritized people. In the spirit of creating an inclusive and democratic understanding of the built environment, it is important to include those who do not conform to heteronormative gender ideals. Otherwise, our study of vernacular architecture reproduces exclusionary systems of power and leaves out an important part of all cultures.

6

RESEARCHING GENDERED EXPERIENCE

Exploring gender in vernacular architecture requires asking questions that focus on the multiple ways that gender engages with the built environment, as we have seen in the last four chapters. Answering these questions requires an expansion of the methods and sources conventionally used in vernacular architecture studies. The methods and sources we use constrain the stories we can tell, and methods are shaped by cultural assumptions about the comparative legitimacy of different kinds of sources; what modes of analysis are considered rigorous; and how to categorize spaces, objects, and activities. For example, the periodization we use to understand prehistory is based on technologies of hunting and cutting tools, from stone to bronze to iron. Feminist archaeologists have pointed out that were we to work from more conventionally feminized technologies such as textiles and ceramics, we might interpret the eras of the past differently.[1] Similarly, categories of private and public, their relationship to gender, and how to understand them in the built environment are predicated on elite, modern White ways of being in the world.[2] Archaeologist Whitney Battle-Baptiste challenges assumptions about the domestic realm in her analysis of enslaved Black homespace, which encompasses exterior spaces like the yard and serves a communal as well as a familial purpose.[3]

Understanding how gender is manifest in the built environment requires us to uncover how both physical space and gender structures were understood by the people who created and used that built environment. We can only understand a ladies' reading room in a library, for instance, by exploring the symbolic and cultural importance of libraries and the constructions of gender that constrain men and women to different spaces within that library. Even more important, but often harder to get at, is how gendered spaces have been experienced. It is through experience that gender structures are made manifest; everyday practice defines and naturalizes what it is to be male and female within a culture. Everyday practice is also where contradictions in gender ideology become visible and where norms of gender can be challenged, whether publicly, as when suffragists gave speeches in public spaces in the early twentieth century, or more privately, as in the homes of many queer families.[4]

Exploring the gendered meanings and experiences of the built environment requires a creative approach to methods and sources. Vernacular architecture scholars often borrow methods and sources from multiple disciplines, focusing on how they can help us interpret buildings and landscapes. For example, we can learn from archaeologists' methods for interpreting material culture as well as how they use other sources such as ethnographies of analogous cultures to enhance their interpretation of the material. We can also learn from sociologists' and anthropologists' use of interviews and ethnography, including participant observation, as tools for getting at both broad cultural ideas and individualized experiences. Approaching both evidence and methods creatively allows us to interpret familiar sources in new ways. In my own research, for example, I used anthropological methods of coding ethnographic data to help me interpret thirty-five years of Annie Haskell's daily diary entries in order to explore her everyday experience of public spaces in San Francisco at the turn of the century. This chapter provides a brief introduction to a wide range of sources and methods, exploring how they are useful for accessing the gendered meanings of the built environment and how buildings and landscapes have been experienced in gendered ways.

Images

Images have long been a core source for vernacular architecture study; historic photographs, for example, communicate a great deal about the form and context of a building in different periods. Sketches, photographs, and measured drawings, and more recently 3D laser scans,

FIG. 6.1. This postcard of the Horn and Hardart Automat, Philadelphia, from before 1907, presents it as an appropriate place for women and families to eat unescorted.

provide information about the details of a building at the time that field research was done, as well as speaking to the priorities of the researchers in the field. But images can also provide important insight into how spaces have been understood and used. Every image tells a story, and we can excavate those stories for cultural information. An important starting point is determining who created an image, why, and for what audience.

Postcards can be understood as a form of advertising created by local boosters and business owners for an audience largely of visitors and potential visitors. Postcards of locations communicate to us about what local leaders of the time thought was most impressive and important, whether a paved parking lot, a substantial brick downtown, or impressive public buildings.[5] Postcards of businesses tell us how the business managers saw themselves and their clientele, and what they

FIG. 6.2. The well-dressed mixed-gender patrons, including women dining alone, featured in this postcard of the Majestic Selfserv in Detroit, c. 1910, suggest that this is a respectable establishment for women and families. The small tables, light bentwood chairs, and tile floor reinforce this message.

saw as their biggest selling point. We can read the images on postcards as evidence of the cultural meanings of places. For example, a pre-1907 postcard of Horn and Hardart's Philadelphia automat (figure 6.1) emphasizes the appropriateness of the automat as a place for unescorted women to eat. It shows two respectably dressed White women, one with a child, at a counter selecting food. The one legible sign within the image proclaims, "Ice Cream," signaling light and sweet food of the sort associated with women diners. The foreground contains an image of a round table that seats four to five, set with a full range of condiments and paired with substantial wooden chairs. This table evokes the idea of "tables for ladies," where women can eat in peace without needing to share space with men. A slightly later (1907–1914) postcard of the Majestic Selfserv in Detroit (figure 6.2) depicts a range of well-dressed White diners, all sitting at small round tables. Many tables have a single diner, male or female, but the tables in the foreground feature couples, with the women's enormous hats tinted pink and blue, drawing the eye. In the background, an unaccompanied woman appears to be paying for her meal, and largely Black staff in uniform stand at attention. These postcards express the novelty of the cafeteria or self-serve restaurant,

FIG. 6.3. This 1940 postcard of the Palm Cafeteria in Clearwater, Florida, does not show patrons, just the many small tables with white tablecloths and lightweight chairs, linoleum floor, and orderly cafeteria line that characterize cafeterias of the period.

formats that were being invented in the early twentieth century and did not yet have a clear cultural meaning.[6] The prominence of women in these images, and particularly unaccompanied women, shows that cafeterias were being actively promoted as safe and appropriate spaces for women to dine alone. Later postcards rarely show patrons, just vast arrays of matching small tables, sometimes with the serving line behind (figure 6.3). This change suggests that by the 1940s, the gendered meaning of the cafeteria was no longer being actively constructed; the appropriateness of its space to men or women dining alone, as well as to families, was common knowledge, and cafeterias sold themselves on neatness, scale, and decoration.

Advertisements and images in magazines similarly speak about broad cultural ideals. For example, the images in mid-1950s *Better Homes and Gardens* clearly express the centrality of the space of the kitchen. Advertisements for appliances, cabinets, and sinks, but also flooring, paint, cleaning products, pipes, and electrical strips, feature colorful spacious kitchens. Notably, nearly every kitchen image features a woman standing in the kitchen cooking (figure 6.4). Even when the kitchen includes a seating area or the woman is drinking

FIG. 6.4. Like most advertisements showing kitchens, this 1959 General Electric advertisement features a well-dressed woman apparently cooking, as well as the turkey and baked goods she has cooked. *Better Homes and Gardens*, Oct. 1959, 29.

FIG. 6.5. In this 1954 American Kitchens advertisement, the apron-clad woman is talking on the phone and there is no food to be seen, but she is still standing in the center of the kitchen. *Better Homes and Gardens*, Aug. 1954, 91.

coffee or talking on the phone, she is standing up (figure 6.5). If the image includes other people, they are nearly always sitting down and are served by the standing woman (figure 6.6). Examining these images in the aggregate, we can understand not only how the kitchen was gendered in the mid-twentieth century US, but also the idealized role of women in the home and the family. These images can help us to interpret the potential gendered meanings of space in an ordinary house of that era.

Personal photographs can tell us about how people have actually used space in ordinary buildings. They show how a space is decorated, how it is populated, and suggest how a person wants to remember it. They can tell us about private lives hidden within otherwise ordinary

FIG. 6.6. In this 1954 Kenflex Vinyl Floor advertisement, a woman is serving a bathrobe-clad man. *Better Homes and Gardens*, Aug. 1954, 30.

apartments. For example, the polaroids taken of lovers and other visitors by Samuel Steward in the early 1950s are interpreted by Stephen Vider as demonstrating a play of erotic fantasy and reality within this queer apartment, where a hidden erotic mural that is exposed by folding down the murphy bed functions as a stage set for attractive nude male bodies.[7] Similarly, photographs of Max Ewing's 1920s–1930s closet "gallery" of clippings and photographs allow Alice Friedman to explore how Ewing created a queer, interracial private space that functioned as part of a larger queer archipelago within New York City.[8] Most personal photographs are more ordinary and attest to the texture of lived experience. For example, a photo of a gathering at Joan Nestle's New York apartment during the 1982 Barnard Conference on Sexuality (figure 6.7) is a haphazardly framed snapshot of a party, with people facing every which way, smiling as they talk with each other. A large image of Radclyffe Hall and a painting of a butch woman, combined with the personal style of the women depicted, suggest that this is a lesbian space. The shelves to the right of the image, filled with binders, are testament to the second identity of this apartment as the original home

FIG. 6.7. This snapshot of Joan Nestle, Deborah Edel, and group at a gathering at Lesbian Herstory Archives/Joan Nestle's apartment on the weekend of the Barnard Conference in April 1982 is not created to make an argument about people or place, but rather to capture an important moment in time. Analyzing the decoration and collections within the space, we can see the fuzzy line between private and community space in this apartment and archive. Photo by Morgan Gwenwald, Lesbian Herstory Archives collections.

of the Lesbian Herstory Archives, a broad-ranging grassroots archive created to save a lesbian history that is not seen through patriarchal eyes.[9] Through examining this and other photos of Nestle's apartment, we can see how this ordinary apartment was simultaneously a home, decorated with images of lesbian identity, and a collective space for community organizing and memory keeping. Photos help us to understand how this apartment was domestic and political, individual and collective, queer and ordinary.

Photographs are very fruitful sources for getting at more ephemeral aspects of the built environment, particularly how spaces are furnished and decorated. Other sources can help fill in the picture photographs begin. Memoirs and interviews can provide rich descriptions, while letters, sales records, and estate inventories give extremely valuable clues as to the material culture contained within a building, and physical traces of wear, paint, and wallpaper give incontrovertible evidence as to aspects of decoration and use.

Material Traces

Buildings are material traces, and vernacular architecture studies has conventionally been based on the recording of buildings. But in addition to the structures themselves, other material traces can tell us about how a building has been used. Stains and markings on walls, patterns of wear, floor coverings, paint, and other traces of use can reveal how a building has been used and reused. Archaeologists can provide models for learning from traces, as their research is typically grounded on the analysis of discarded objects. The types of objects discarded and their spatial distribution can provide important insight into gendered use of space. For example, the objects found in three 1870–1910 privies associated with a schoolhouse in rural Indiana allowed archaeologists to determine that one privy was used by females and the other two were used by males. The male privies contained objects that might easily have fallen out of pockets, such as hex nuts, pocketknives, marbles, and rubber balls. In contrast, the female privy contained primarily domestic objects, including ceramic sherds, broken glass containers, metal food containers, and a knife and spoon. The archaeologists argued that the objects found in the female privies suggested that women and girls likely were responsible for serving and cleaning up at community social events, which other evidence suggested the school was used for. The objects in the privy tell us both about the organization of male and female space and also about male and female gendered roles. Other evidence at the site, including a large number of munitions artifacts near a tree that may have been used for skill-shooting games and a concentration of straight pins, a needle, and a safety pin near one corner of the building suggest gendered use of the space surrounding the school.[10]

Material traces can also suggest ways that gender is performed and constructed. Excavation of the Zeta Psi fraternity at the University of California provided clues as to the ways that young men constructed masculinity within an all-male community. The remains of matching white plates and mugs found in association with their first, pre-1910 fraternity house are interpreted by archaeologist Laurie Wilkie as a sign that the fraternity brothers were symbolically constituting themselves as a family, using the same material culture that their mothers used to express family unity and purity in the homes they grew up in. Their privileged class position was marked through the remains of highly decorative lamp chimneys, while their concern with their personal appearance was expressed through gold-plated buttons, porcelain cuff links, toiletry bottles, and deodorant jars. Their use of space was also suggested by the remains of beer bottles, wine bottles, beer mugs, and goblets in the area of their roomy front porch, suggesting that not only did they drink, but they drank in a public and sociable context on the threshold of public space.[11]

While archaeologists typically rely on excavations to provide traces of use, many traces can be discovered without digging. Graffiti, for instance, can tell us about people's use of spaces as well as the ways they conceptualize themselves, other users, and the space itself. Sociologist Pamela Leong examined graffiti in men's and women's university bathrooms to explore how public bathrooms function as sites of gender performance and conformity. She found that graffiti in women's bathrooms was often relationship oriented, with largely supportive responses. This, combined with women's posts about their bodies, suggests that the privacy of the stall within the female-only space of the bathroom was experienced by women as a refuge. In contrast, in the men's bathroom the combination of anonymity and publicity encouraged a performance of an insult-based, sexual, macho masculine identity through graffiti.[12]

Written Documents

A wide range of documents can be read to learn about the gendered meanings of a building or type of place and how it has been experienced as gendered. These vary from written records to novels, journals, letters, and diaries. Vernacular architecture scholars have long used probate documents to discover what objects were kept in each room of a house, using these as clues to the ways that people lived within a building, with the sorts of furniture and other valuable items listed suggesting what kinds of activities took place in each room as well as the lifestyle of the occupants. The manuscript census can give us insight into households, informing us about the official familial relationships between household members, and letting us know the nature of households: whether nuclear or multigenerational, and whether they included more distant relations or unrelated friends, roomers, and boarders. Mapping households onto building form, we can begin to ask questions about how space might have been used and about the relationship between house forms and household structures.

Guidebooks and etiquette books are windows into gendered ideals. Reading San Francisco guidebooks, I found that the downtown was imagined as two separate gendered realms, one a masculine landscape of business and purpose, the other a feminine landscape of consumption, leisure, and frivolity. Actual lived experience did not match up fully with these ideals, as I discovered by mapping businesses in both landscapes and through diary entries describing women's visits downtown. However, this ideal gendering influenced how spaces were decorated and experienced; and it helps to explain the turn-of-the-century architectural type which isolated feminine shops and masculine offices from each other within the same building, such that to go from one to the other, one would need to go out onto the sidewalk.[13] Etiquette books are similarly windows into gendered ideals and provide insight into the gendered rituals that enliven a space, such as the rituals of carving and serving meat on elaborate dining-room sideboards or the family procession to honor the ancestors in a late imperial Chinese home. They do not necessarily reflect actual practice, but they communicate about changes and cultural anxieties. For example, in a survey of late nineteenth- and early twentieth-century etiquette books, I found that gendered behavior on streetcars was a source of contention. In the nineteenth-century books, men were instructed to give their seats to women as to do otherwise was ungentlemanly, but by the early twentieth century, while authors still agreed women should have the seats, the etiquette advice was focused more on the rudeness of women who demanded them rather than the men who should cede them. The logic also shifted to one of need rather than of gender alone, and one writer even suggested that sometimes a tired male worker needed a seat more than an elite woman. I argue that this shift in etiquette is not only reflective of women's increasing ridership of streetcars, but also of a shift in understanding of womanhood, in which women are no longer seen as inherently frail nor inherently out of place in public space. This cultural shift maps with changes in the design of San Francisco streetcars in 1911, in which front-facing seats were replaced with long benches on either side of the car. Reading the design of streetcars through the lens of etiquette books allows us to see this change as reflective, in part, of a shift in gender ideology.[14]

We can also see gendered ideals through instructional literature, including decorating manuals, trade journals, and professional manuals. These sources can be particularly useful for exploring institutional and architectural types, such as libraries, summer camps, YMCAs, and Masonic lodges.[15] Instructional books, histories of individual institutions, and journals published by organizations all give evidence as to the dominant ideas about the uses and meanings of space, ways that space may be used counter to those ideas, and details of spatial organization and decoration. How-to guides for houses, from Confucian manuals to Victorian builders' guides to contemporary television shows and articles on interior decoration, can be a core source for interpreting houses through a gendered lens because they articulate not only how homes should be built and lived in, but why.

Trade journals similarly give us a top-down view of how a certain kind of space is organized and used, who the users are assumed to be, and what aspects of use are seen as problematic. For example, retail grocers' publications in the early twentieth century worked to promote an ideal of grocers as professional and scientific and decidedly male, even as they acknowledged the existence of female grocers. Highly orderly interiors, quite different from the elaborate and overwhelming department store interiors of the same era, reinforced this image of a rational, scientific space (figure 6.8). How grocers and shoppers are written about in trade journals, and the advice and images of ideal store displays, provide details about how gender was understood within corner groceries and what the spaces might have been like for those who experienced them.[16]

The records of social reformers, charitable organizations, and the police can all be read against the grain as clues to the experiences of poor people, single people, queer people, and others that the dominant class saw as nonconforming. To write about the lives of working-class women in Boston at the turn of the century, Sarah Deutsch made use of the case records of settlement houses and other charitable organizations. These records provide detailed information on individual lives that she used to construct an understanding not only of working-class women's experiences, but also of their spatial and social strategies for survival.[17] Similarly, the sources George Chauncey uses to explore the lives of gay men in early twentieth-century New York include police reports, court records, and the records of organizations investigating vice.[18] The limit of these sorts of sources, of course, is that they speak from an outsider's point of view, and one that is quite partial and prejudiced. It is important to read these reports with a consciousness of their writers' points of view, and to complement them as much as possible with letters, interviews, and other firsthand accounts.

Diaries and letters are a window into firsthand experience, although they are not always written in a way that is easily deciphered. Diaries, in particular, are written for an audience of one, and only rarely explain or describe, except when writing about unusual experiences, such as travels. However, they can be rich sources on experience, letting us know, for example, how the same downtown department stores were experienced by an elite woman as a space of comfort and by a less well-to-do one as a site of frustration. They give us access to emotion and often to intimate aspects of everyday life that otherwise remain hidden, as in the diaries of gay life in New York used as sources by Chauncey.[19] Diaries can also give us details about how a house is lived in, ones that are not captured in censuses and formal documents. For example, the early twentieth-century diaries of Annie Haskell let us know that the lower-middle-class household she was part of in San Francisco included her sister and family, Annie and her son, a girl from their hometown who was working in a department store, and a boy from next door, who slept in their kitchen because there was not enough room for him to sleep in his own home.[20] Similarly, diaries and letters provide details on complexly changing families based on plural marriages in late nineteenth-century Utah, giving Thomas Carter insight into the housing choices made by polygamist families as well as how a given house could be used to accommodate various family forms.[21]

Letters and postcards can be similarly intimate, relying upon the knowledge shared between the writer and the addressee. They usually explain and describe more than diaries do and can thus be a rich source for discovering experience. For example, George Chauncey uses the letters of Parker Tyler, which describe gay social encounters in the 1920s in detail, activities that were more often hidden.[22] Postcards have minimal space for text in comparison to letters, but the pairing of image and text is evocative, and postcard collections can provide an opportunity to compare large numbers of messages written by ordinary people whose letters and other documents are less likely to be saved in archives. Paula Lupkin's analysis of YMCA postcard collections explores how messages on postcards, in reassuring family that the writer was safe and well, assumed an understanding of the YMCA as a safe and reassuring place, one that created a safe framework for flirtation between young people.[23]

Memoirs and novels are written for a broad public audience and therefore contain much more explicit description, although they also need to be understood as interpretations and representations of culture, not as pure descriptions of personal experience. They both express gendered ideals and describe experience and thus can be used as a source for both aspects of gendered space. To analyze how students experienced women's colleges, Helen Horowitz uses novels, short stories, and letters, which provide insight into spatial social stratification and the use of dorm rooms as parlors for private entertaining.[24] Novels and memoirs can also attest to collective memory; archaeologist Whitney Battle-Baptiste found that fiction and memoirs by Black women expressed important aspects of Black women's historical and contemporary experience, particularly about the ways that gender articulates with race, opening up space for her archaeological interpretations with that tradition at its core.[25]

Films similarly express spatially located gender ideals and conflicts, and their depictions of spaces and the experience of spaces is very rich, allowing scholars to analyze close details of décor and the ways spaces are used. For example, film scholar Pamela Wojcik explores gender, race, and the meanings of the apartment in the mid-twentieth century by analyzing popular film and television depictions of the apartments of single men, single women, White families, and Black professional families. Films allow her to analyze the details of organization and decoration in single women's shared bohemian apartments, for example, and to contrast them to the spaciousness and high design of filmic bachelor pads.[26]

Less formal written records can be extremely useful for exploring aspects of the use of space. For example, Daphne Spain made use of flyers asking for donations of furniture to help get a sense of how the Crenshaw Women's Center was furnished. She also read the Women's Center's archives for information that she could analyze to get clues about furniture and the use of space. Information sent to women going to a counselor training session, for example, advised them to bring pillows to sit on, suggesting that the procurement of furniture was still unfinished.[27] Flyers, zines, and similar ephemera have also been important sources for the history of queer spaces.[28]

Oral Histories and Interviews

One of the richest possible sources for exploring how a space is experienced is firsthand description, often obtained through oral histories and interviews. Interviews and oral histories are particularly useful for accessing the experience of people underrepresented in the official record, including immigrants, racial minorities, the poor, women, and queer folk, and are thus particularly useful for exploring questions of gender and sexuality in the built environment.[29] Interviews and oral histories are particularly fruitful sources for determining who has shaped the built environment as well as how it is used. Both oral histories and other kinds of interviews are based on asking a person questions and recording their answers. The main distinction between them is that oral histories are longer and more directed by the narrator; they allow a person time to tell what is most important to them rather than answering a specific set of questions.[30] Sometimes oral histories are quite open ended, functioning very much like oral memoirs, while others are more clearly focused on the narrator's relationship to a particular aspect of their life, such as a political or religious movement they participated in. Oral histories give a broad overview and can be extremely rich. They also give significant agency to the narrator and can thus provide nuanced and rich information that may sometimes challenge a researcher's assumptions more than an interview with set questions. In addition, there are many oral history projects that include interviews with people who lived as early as the nineteenth century, and these can be used to access a deeper history than is possible with currently living people.[31]

In comparison to oral histories, interviews are usually focused on a specific question and can go into detail about a specific building or place. They are thus uniquely important for studies such as Brent Pilkey's exploration of queer self-expression in home decoration and David Brody's analysis of hotel spaces from the point of view of the women who clean them, both of which require a focus on spaces and practices that might not be discussed in an oral history.[32] Interviews are one of the best ways to get at how a space is actually used as opposed to how it is culturally intended to be used. Through interviews with the inhabitants of a mid-twentieth-century suburban Eichler home, Annmarie Adams discovered the many ways that one relatively typical family's practices defied the ideal norms presented in advertising and home magazines. For example, although the house was designed so that the mother in the kitchen could watch over children playing in the backyard and front atrium, the children played on the street, in the garage, and in a hidden side yard, and the atrium was used to store bicycles rather than as a place to play. This information about behavior is not easily visible in the built landscape; it is only through interviews and the analysis of snapshots that Adams was able to describe the experienced domestic landscape of these ordinary women and children.[33] Interviews can combine the oral and other media; in her study of cleaning and decorating practices and gender, anthropologist Sarah Pink combined tape-recorded interviews about gender identity and lifestyle with videotaped house tours narrated by her interviewees. The video format resulted in the collection of visual and contextual information beyond words and allowed the interviewees a great deal of leeway in narrating their own experience of their home and what mattered most to them within it.[34]

Participant Observation

The ethnographic method of participant observation entails participating in the culture being studied, learning its rules and norms first-hand. Vernacular architecture scholars can make use of participant observation to access the complexities of lived experience, including changes in the use of a space over the course of a day, week, and year; multisensory aspects of experience including smell and sound; and the ways that the space is transformed through the performance of everyday life. Observing and participating are core methods for discovering the ways everyday life is enacted. Vernacular architecture comes to life through everyday experience, and many argue that the experience is as important as the building itself. Scholars of ethnic neighborhoods have argued that by focusing on how buildings are used and transformed, rather than on their origins, we can begin to understand the vernacular architecture of the less powerful, whether the Latinx populations of Chicago's Little Village or the South Asian denizens of Devon Avenue in Chicago.[35] A focus on everyday life is similarly essential for understanding gender and sexuality in vernacular architecture, for it is through how a space is used and understood that it participates in the construction and enactment of gender.

Participant observation can begin with something as simple as spending time in a place, noticing the everyday ballet of people's actions and interactions within it, and attentively using all one's senses to take in the sounds, smells, tastes, and bodily sensations it offers. A more immersive engagement may involve living and/or working within a community. Being a participant also opens space for a collaborative form of research in which, rather than extracting information from community members, the researchers work with them to build knowledge together. While this type of research takes time, it centers the understandings and priorities of the members of a community and leads to a much richer understanding of the significance of vernacular buildings and landscapes.[36]

Storytelling

Not only the sources we use, but also the way we write about them can have consequences for addressing gender in the built environment. Many feminist scholars have argued that we can tell a fuller, more peopled history by experimenting with alternative modes of writing that go beyond the abstract and the impersonal. In *What this Awl Means,* archaeologist Janet Spector challenges the scientific classificatory approach to analyzing and writing about archaeological data. She begins with a small antler awl handle inscribed with dots and lines that she excavated at a Wahpeton Lakota site in Minnesota and uses it as the basis of a descriptive story that puts the awl into context as a symbolically significant tool for a young Wahpeton woman, on which she marked her completion of beaded and quilled projects. Every aspect of the story is based on research, but it is presented in a way that brings the reader emotionally into the experience rather than maintaining a distance. This rejection of the scientific, objective "view from above" is grounded in a long discussion in feminist philosophy on the ways that the viewpoint of the observer affects what is seen.[37] In *Black Feminist Archaeology*, Whitney Battle-Baptiste pulls together her own embodied experience in the field, the results of her fieldwork, what she has learned from her own upbringing as a Black woman, and conversations with her elders in her archaeological interpretation of the Hermitage site, making a convincing argument for the importance of bringing one's personal experience into analysis.[38]

Both Spector and Battle-Baptiste imaginatively project themselves into a time or culture separate from their own, although they do it with caution and based on rigorous research. While this approach is not without peril, this sort of imaginative experience can be generative of new understandings of the built environment. For example, a gendered analysis of the early twentieth-century grocery store could start from

FIG. 6.8. In late nineteenth- and early twentieth-century grocery stores, most products were served to patrons by the grocer, who kept goods behind a counter. This highly orderly space was controlled by the shopkeeper. Early twentieth-century photograph of a grocery store interior. Janice Waltzer from Owasso, USA, CC BY 2.0, Wikimedia Commons.

imagining the experience of both the shopper and the grocer. In the earliest decades of the twentieth century, the shopping experience is one of asking and being served. The shopper, nearly always female, would enter the store and ask for each product, which would be either taken from shelves behind the counter or measured from bins by the grocer (figure 6.8). This is a space in which control resides in the grocer, often, although not always, male, while the female shopper is served. It reinforces female passivity, as the shopper can remain still at the counter as the grocer fulfills her requests. In 1916 this model is challenged by the self-serve Piggly Wiggly, in which shoppers enter the store through a turnstile, pick up a basket, and go through a maze of shelving, picking items off the shelf (figure 6.9). This store changes the experience of the shopper, who now moves actively through the space, making decisions, but at the same time lugging groceries as they go. The grocery clerk's position is deskilled, no longer requiring knowledge of products,

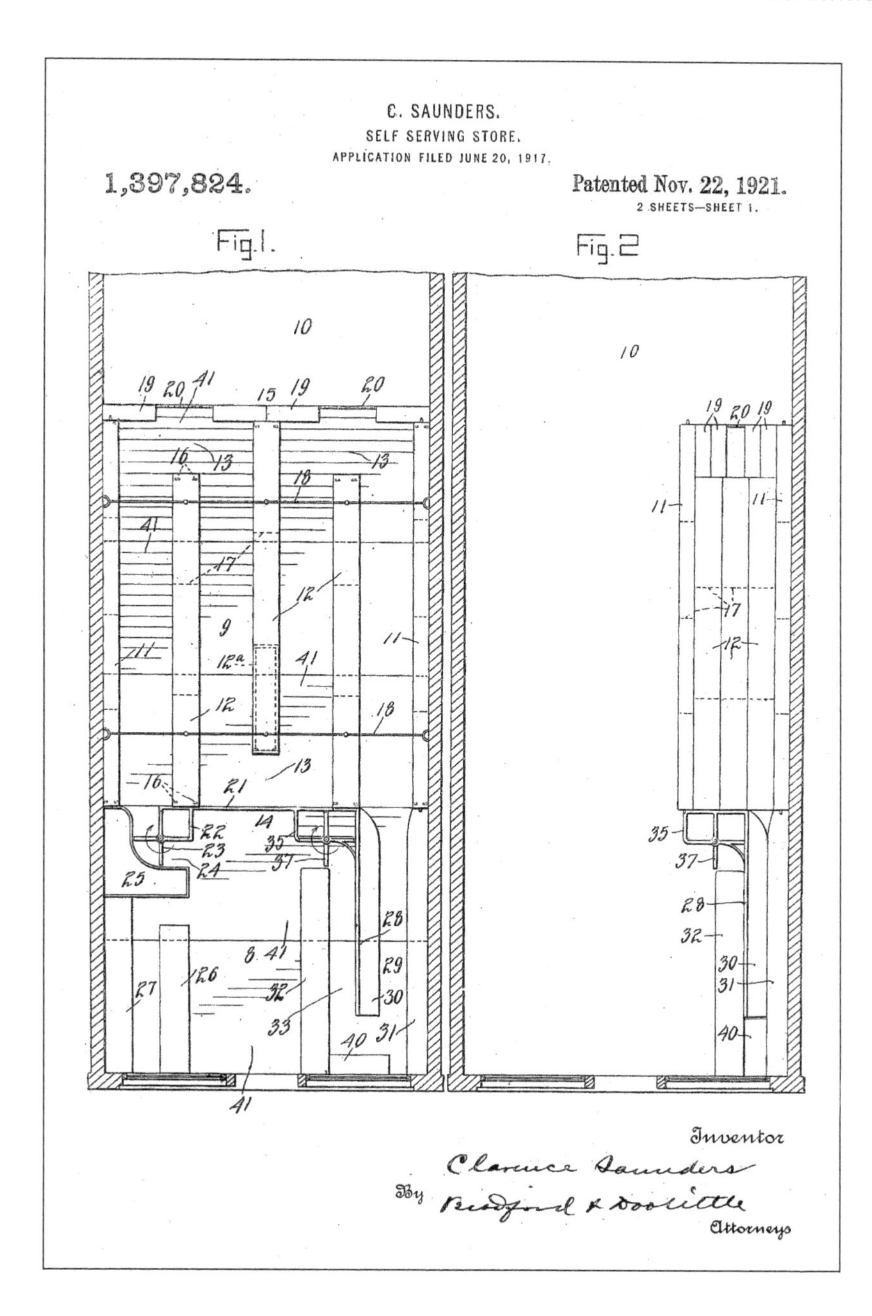

FIG. 6.9. In the Piggly Wiggly, a shopper zigzags past all the shelves in the store, a design which was patented. This shifted the experience of the shopper, who now served herself, making decisions as to brands and products independently. Patent 1397824, patented Nov. 22, 1921.

nor physical effort, but merely the ability to run a cash register (figure 6.10). This new cashier position also becomes increasingly feminized. Imagining the bodily and psychological experience of the old and new grocery helps open up ways of interpreting the self-serve grocery store not just as a new model of efficiency, but one that depends on changing gender ideals.

FIG. 6.10. In the Piggly Wiggly, shown here in 1918, the grocer is no longer an expert doling out goods, but rather a clerk ringing up purchases. Photograph by Clarence Saunders, Public domain, Wikimedia Commons.

Combining Methods

No one source tells a full story. Doing research on gender in vernacular architecture requires making use of a range of sources and weaving the findings from each of them together. The social sciences use the term triangulation to refer to using multiple methods, observers, and sources in order to overcome problems of intrinsic bias. When studying gender in vernacular architecture, we should ideally use multiple sources and methods to understand how a building or landscape is imagined or understood as gendered and how it is experienced, as well as its physical form and any changes that may have been made. We may find that different methods tell similar stories but fill in the picture more fully. Or we may discover that there are contradictions between ideals and experience, or between ideals and built form, challenging us to understand why. While physical form is always important, we always need to make use of a range of sources and methods that activate that form and help us understand how it is experienced in order to tell a story about gender.

CONCLUSION

THE FUTURE OF VERNACULAR ARCHITECTURE STUDIES

In this book I argue for a nuanced approach to power and experience in studies of vernacular architecture and cultural landscapes. In order to see gender and sexuality in the built environment, we need to start from the understanding that cultures are never unified, such that every person within them has the same beliefs and practices. Each individual has their own agency and individuality, but they are also influenced by their position within a culture. Youths may have different beliefs and knowledges than the elderly, for example. To explore gender and sexuality, we need to pay attention to the differences within a culture as much as the norms of the culture overall.

Cultures are also always structures of power. Cultural norms provide a general outline of who has what kind of power and in what circumstances. But power is contested and complex; it does not just follow the rules. We need to understand the rules: to understand gender, we need to recognize the workings of patriarchy; to understand sexuality, we need to see heteronormativity; to understand race, we need to examine racial hierarchies and White supremacy. But we should not stop with the norms, we should also pay attention to how and when those norms are followed, adjusted, or ignored. It is important not to assume that anything or anyone that resists the norms is somehow outside a culture; a culture is made up not only of those with power, but also of those who use the weapons of the weak, contesting, subverting, and even changing the norms.

While norms are often visibly built into the physical environment, we can only fully understand their complexity by also examining experience. It is through experience that norms become naturalized; when spaces are regularly divided by gender or race, it can feel as though the differences they enact are innate and self-evident. But it is also through experience that norms are transformed. Sometimes different aspects of a culture contradict each other, leading to a cultural change. For example, in the late nineteenth century, the growing feminized retail world of department stores and downtown shops in the US and Europe put women downtown in public spaces that older, but still powerful, gender norms had marked as male. That contradiction, I have argued, helped transform gendered norms in Western cultures.[1] Examining lived experience also gives us insight into other ways that everyday practices can challenge and transform cultural norms, for example, by turning an apartment into an archive, a bookstore into a feminist refuge, or a suburban home into a space for a nontraditional family. We need to take experience seriously in order to understand how buildings and landscapes function as part of the lives of all members of society, not just the most powerful.

I argue that to study gender well, we need to approach vernacular architecture as entwined with power and understood through experience. Taking this approach will not only help us to see gender better but will also enrich all aspects of our understanding of the ordinary built environment. Like gender, race, class, sexuality, and ethnicity are not only identities, but also structures of power that are built into our buildings and landscapes, and the same tools that help us see gender can enrich our exploration of them. Exploring how cultural categories like gender, class, and race are built into our physical world, and also how they are enacted, transformed, and resisted through individual experience, will allow us to see every aspect of vernacular architecture, and all buildings and landscapes, more fully.

Vernacular architecture is the spaces in which we live our lives. We experience these spaces as gendered beings, and the spaces express and shape ideas about what it is to be gendered beings. To truly understand these spaces, we need to use a gendered lens, one that approaches gender intersectionally, so that we ask not just about how a given example of vernacular architecture shapes and reflects gender, but also how the gender it shapes is defined by class, race, and many other categories. To study vernacular architecture, I would argue, requires studying gender. Without it, our view of the built environment is partial and likely biased.

In this book, we have seen that studying gender requires paying close attention to how vernacular architecture is experienced and used. We cannot stop at how a building is built; we need to also ask about how it has been changed, how it has been inhabited, and how it has been understood. Taking this broad approach to where meaning resides in the built environment not only allows us to see gender better, but it also makes ethnicity, sexuality, race, age, and other aspects of culture more visible and allows us to see how they imprint themselves in vernacular architecture, whether through ways of inhabiting space, modes of decoration and spatial organization, or ephemeral events that transform a space's meanings even if just for one night. This approach allows us to see how buildings are layered and multiple — they express those who thought them up, those who built them, those who inhabited them, and those who encountered them. All these stories are part of their meanings and their histories, and all of them matter. Vernacular architecture studies that is grounded in attention to gender and to the multiple meanings embodied in the built environment is more inclusive, truer, and more multifaceted than one that stays tied to the physical traces of the building alone. Still rooted in the building as a physical artifact, it allows us to explore how the building and its meaning interact, to give us a fuller picture of building as culture.

Reading this book has given you some tools to enhance your understanding of the buildings and landscapes you live in and study. I hope I have encouraged you to dig deeply from multiple disciplines. You can learn from scholars who are interested in similar questions, even if their scholarship does not have any obvious ties to the built environment. I also hope that your future vernacular architecture studies will address questions of gender and power even when your focus is not explicitly on gender, so that we can better understand the immense diversity of experience of the built environment and how different dimensions of power play out within our physical world.

Notes

CHAPTER ONE

1. In 2007, the Vernacular Architecture Forum changed the name of its journal from *Perspectives in Vernacular Architecture* to *Buildings and Landscapes*, reflecting the expansion of focus from buildings alone to cultural landscapes as well. Dell Upton, in "The VAF at 25: What Now?" *Perspectives in Vernacular Architecture* 13, no. 2 (2006–7): 7, writes that "vernacular architecture" is "shorthand for 'vernacular architecture, cultural landscapes, and material culture.'" This overlap is made clear by the collection *Everyday America: Cultural Landscape Studies After J. B. Jackson* (Berkeley: University of California Press, 2003), edited by Chris Wilson and Paul Groth, both scholars of vernacular architecture and stalwarts of the Vernacular Architecture Forum.

2. Camille Wells, "Old Claims and New Demands: Vernacular Architecture Studies Today," in *Perspectives in Vernacular Architecture* 2, ed. Camille Wells (Columbia: University of Missouri Press, 1986), 1–10; Thomas Carter and Elizabeth Collins Cromley, *Invitation to Vernacular Architecture: A Guide to the Study of Ordinary Buildings and Landscapes* (Knoxville: University of Tennessee Press, 2005), especially 7–18; Upton, "The VAF at 25"; Jeffrey E. Klee, "Viewpoint: Fieldwork, Mind, and Building," *Buildings and Landscapes* 25, no. 2 (Fall 2018): 1–16.

3. Thomas Carter and Bernard L. Herman, "Introduction: Towards a New Architectural History," in *Perspectives in Vernacular Architecture* 4, ed. Thomas Carter and Bernard L. Herman (Columbia: University of Missouri Press, 1991), 1–6.

4. For example, of the seventeen papers and five abstracts in *Perspectives in Vernacular Architecture* 1, ed. Camille Wells (Columbia: University of Missouri Press, 1982), most focus on regionally specific building forms, but one has an additional focus on women and another on Black settlements. Elizabeth Collins Cromley and Carter L. Hudgins's (eds.) *Perspectives in Vernacular Architecture 5: Gender, Class, and Culture* (Knoxville: University of Tennessee Press, 1995) explicitly addresses gender and other aspects of difference, with four of its eighteen articles explicitly addressing gender and three focusing on race and ethnicity. In that volume, Angel Kwolek-Folland's "Gender as a Category of Analysis in Vernacular Architecture Studies," 3–10, makes a cogent argument against an "add women and stir" approach to gender, while Deryck W. Holdsworth's "'I'm a Lumberjack and I'm OK': The Built Environment and Varied Masculinities in the Industrial Age," 11–25, is unusual in its focus on masculinity. Another significant addition to the twentieth-century discourse on gender

in vernacular architecture studies is Sally McMurry's "Women in the American Vernacular Landscape," *Material Culture* 20:1 (Spring 1988), 33-49.

5. Anna Andrzejewski, "*Perspectives in Vernacular Architecture*, the VAF and the Study of Ordinary Buildings and Landscapes in North America," *Perspectives in Vernacular Architecture* 13, no. 2 (2006–7): 58.

6. Henry Glassie, *Material Culture* (Bloomington: Indiana University Press, 1999), 41.

7. Jules David Prown, "Mind in Matter: An Introduction to Material Culture Theory and Method," *Winterthur Portfolio* 17, no. 1 (Spring 1982): 1–19; Henry Glassie, "Meaningful Things and Appropriate Myths: The Artifact's Place in American Studies," in *Prospects: An Annual of American Cultural Studies*, ed. Jack Salzman, vol. 3 (New York: Burt Franklin, 1978), 1–49.

8. Carter and Cromley, *Invitation to Vernacular Architecture*, xiii; Glassie, *Material Culture*.

9. Pierce Lewis, "Axioms for Reading the Landscape: Some Guides to the American Scene," in *The Interpretation of Ordinary Landscapes: Geographical Essays*, ed. D. W. Meinig (Oxford: Oxford University Press, 1979), 18–19.

10. Annette Weiner, *Women of Value; Men of Renown: New Perspectives in Trobriand Exchange* (Austin: University of Texas Press, 1976).

11. See Carter and Cromley, *Invitation to Vernacular Architecture*, 11–12.

12. The Vernacular Architecture Forum (VAF) was born out of a 1979 symposium on vernacular architecture hosted by the Graduate Program in Historic Preservation at George Washington University, which also hosted the first meeting of the VAF in 1980. Warren R. Hofstra and Camille Wells, "Embracing Our Legacy, Shaping Our Future: The Vernacular Architecture Forum Turns Twenty-Five," *Perspectives in Vernacular Architecture* 13, no. 2 (2006–7): 3. Folklorists were particularly prominent in the early years of the VAF. Anna Andrzejewski, "*Perspectives in Vernacular Architecture*, the VAF and the Study of Ordinary Buildings and Landscapes in North America," 58.

13. Henry Glassie, *Folk Housing in Middle Virginia* (Knoxville: University of Tennessee Press, 1975); John Vlach, "The Shotgun House: An African Architectural Legacy: Part One," *Pioneer America* 8, no. 1 (January 1976): 47–60; John Vlach, "The Shotgun House: An African Architectural Legacy: Part Two," *Pioneer America* 8, no. 2 (July 1976): 57–70.

14. Wells, "Old Claims and New Demands," describes Kniffen as the "father" of vernacular architecture studies; Fred B. Kniffen, "Folk Housing: Key to Diffusion," *Annals of the Association of American Geographers* 55 (1965): 549–77, republished in Dell Upton and John Michael Vlach, eds., *Common Places: Readings in American Vernacular Architecture* (Athens: University of Georgia Press, 1986), 3–26.

15. Arijit Sen, "Viewpoint: Spatial Ethnography of Devon Avenue, Chicago," *Buildings and Landscapes* 28, no. 2 (Fall 2021): 3–24. Dell Upton critiques this materialist focus as fetishizing the building as a relic. Upton, "The VAF at 25," 9.

16. Andrew Sandoval-Strauss, "Viewpoint: Latino Vernaculars and the Emerging National Landscape," *Buildings and Landscapes* 20, no. 1 (Spring 2013): 1–18.

17. For example, in *Invitation to Vernacular Architecture*, all non-fieldwork methods are described as "techniques and procedures for elaborating the field data with supplementary historical information." Carter and Cromley, *Invitation to Vernacular Architecture*, 47.

18. Joan Wallach Scott, "Gender: A Useful Category of Social Analysis," *American Historical Review* 91, no. 5 (1986): 1053–75.

19. Erik Erikson, "Sex Differences in the Play Configurations of Preadolescents," *American Journal of Orthopsychiatry* 21 (1951): 667–93. Several later studies contradicted his findings, including Barbara Budd, Pauline Rose Clance, and D. Emily Simerly, "Spatial Configurations: Erikson Reexamined," *Sex Roles* 12, no. 5/6 (1985): 571–77.

20. Biological sex can be defined through multiple criteria, which do not always align. In addition to defining sex through genitalia, gonads, and secondary sexual characteristics, sex can also be defined through chromosomes and by the balance of hormones in the body. The binary understanding of sex is challenged by the existence of the intersexed, people whose biological markers of sex do not align with the binary male/female. See Suzanne J. Kessler, *Lessons from the Intersexed* (New Brunswick, NJ: Rutgers University Press, 1998); Alice Dreger, *Hermaphrodites and the Medical Invention of Sex* (Cambridge, MA: Harvard University Press, 2000).

21. Kimberlé Crenshaw, *On Intersectionality: Essential Writings* (New York: New Press, 2017); Patricia Hill Collins, *Intersectionality as Critical Social Theory* (Durham, NC: Duke University Press, 2019); Patricia Hill Collins, *Black Feminist Thought: Knowledge, Consciousness, and the Politics of Empowerment* (New York: Routledge, 2000).

22. Sojourner Truth, "Ain't I a Woman?" (speech delivered to the Women's Convention, Akron, Ohio, 1851). Modern History Sourcebook, Fordham University, https://sourcebooks.fordham.edu/mod/sojtruth-woman.asp. There are multiple versions of this speech published; this is the version that has circulated most widely, although it is likely not the most accurate version of her actual words.

23. Bell Hooks, *Ain't I a Woman: Black Women and Feminism* (Boston: South End Press, 1981).

24. Jo B. Paoletti, *Pink and Blue: Telling the Boys from the Girls in America* (Bloomington: Indiana University Press, 2012); Tom Shakespeare, "Disabled Sexuality: Toward Rights and Recognition," *Sexuality and Disability* 18, no. 3 (2000): 159–66; David Gissen, *The Architecture of Disability: Buildings, Cities, and Landscapes beyond Access* (Minneapolis: University of Minnesota Press, 2022); Jos Boys, ed., *Disability, Space, Architecture: A Reader* (London: Routledge, 2017); Marta Gutman and Ning de Coninck-Smith, *Designing Modern*

Childhoods: History, Space, and the Material Culture of Children (New Brunswick, NJ: Rutgers University Press, 2008).

25. Kate Bornstein, *My Gender Workbook: How to Become a Real Man, a Real Woman, the Real You, or Something Else Entirely* (New York: Routledge, 1998), 28. This approach is at the center of much contemporary activism and many recent books, such as Meg-John Barker and Jules Scheele, *Gender: A Graphic Guide* (London: Icon Books, 2019).

26. Judith Butler, *Gender Trouble: Feminism and the Subversion of Identity* (New York: Routledge, 1990).

27. For an overview of twentieth-century approaches to exploring the relationship between gender and the built environment, see Jane Rendell, Barbara Penner, and Iain Borden, eds., *Gender Space Architecture: An Interdisciplinary Introduction* (New York: Routledge, 2000). Some of the significant collections looking at gender and architecture (focusing primarily on the non-vernacular) include Diana Agrest, Patricia Conway, and Leslie Kanes Weisman, eds., *The Sex of Architecture* (New York: Harry N. Abrams, Inc., 1996); Debra Coleman, Elizabeth Danze, and Carol Henderson, eds., *Architecture and Feminism* (New York: Princeton Architectural Press, 1996); Duncan McCorquodale, Katerina Ruedi, and Sarah Wigglesworth, eds., *Designing Practices: Architecture, Gender, and the Interdisciplinary* (London: Black Dog Publishing, 1996); Francesca Hughes, ed., *The Architect: Reconstructing Her Practice* (Cambridge, MA: MIT Press, 1996); Louise Durning and Richard Wrigley, eds., *Gender and Architecture* (Chichester: Wiley, 2000); James Benedict Brown, Harriet Harriss, Ruth Morrow, and James Soane, eds., *A Gendered Profession: The Question of Representation in Space Making* (London: RIBA Publishing, 2016); and Hélène Frichot, Catharina Gabrielsson, and Helen Bunting, eds., *Architecture and Feminisms: Ecologies, Economies,* Technologies (New York: Routledge, 2017).

28. Iris Marion Young, "Throwing Like a Girl: A Phenomenology of Feminine Body Comportment Motility and Spatiality," *Human Studies* 3 (1980): 137–56.

CHAPTER TWO

1. Rewriting the history of architecture was part of the project of the pathbreaking Susanna Torre, ed., *Women in American Architecture: A Historic and Contemporary Perspective* (New York: Whitney Library of Design, 1977) and several of the pieces in *Making Room: Women and Architecture, Heresies* 11, vol. 3, no. 3, 1981. It has been continued in monographs on women architects; by the work of Milka Bliznakov and the International Archive of Women in Architecture, which she founded in 1985; and by recent broad collections, including Lori Brown and Karen Burns, eds., *Global Encyclopedia of Women in Architecture* (London: Bloomsbury, 2024) and Anna Sokolina, ed., *The Routledge Companion to Women in Architecture* (London: Routledge, 2024).

2. The pioneering books on Julia Morgan and Eileen Gray are Sara Holmes Boutelle, *Julia Morgan, Architect* (New York: Abbeville Press, 1995) and Peter

Adam, *Eileen Gray: Architect/Designer* (New York: H. N. Abrams, 1987). There have since been multiple books on both architects, including children's books and graphic novels. Some recent books on women in the profession include Jan Hartman, ed. *The Women Who Changed Architecture* (New York: Princeton Architectural Press, 2022); Marcia Feuerstein, Paula Zellner Bassett, and Jodi La Coe, *Expanding Field of Architecture: Women in Architecture Across the Globe* (London: Lund Humphries, 2022); Ursula Schwitalla, ed., *Women in Architecture: Past, Present, and Future* (Berlin: Hatje Cantz Verlag, 2021); and Jane Hall, *Breaking Ground: Architecture by Women* (New York: Phaidon, 2019).

3. See, for example, Jennifer Bloomer, "Big Jugs," in *The Hysterical Male: New Feminist Theory*, ed. Arthur Kroker and Marilouise Kroker (London: Macmillan, 1991), 13–27, and Diana Agrest, *Architecture from Without: Framings for a Critical Practice* (Cambridge, MA: MIT Press, 1991).

4. Karen A. Franck, "A Feminist Approach to Architecture: Acknowledging Women's Ways of Knowing," in *Architecture: A Place for Women*, ed. Ellen Perry Berkeley and Matilda McQuaid (Washington, DC: Smithsonian Institution Press, 1989).

5. Alice T. Friedman, *Women and the Making of the Modern House* (New York: Harry N. Abrams, 1998).

6. Kathleen James-Chakraborty, "Expanding Agency: Women and Modern Architecture and Design" (lecture at Yan P. Lin Centre, McGill University, February 21, 2022).

7. Rina Swentzell, "Conflicting Landscape Values: The Santa Clara Pueblo and Day School," *Places* 7, no. 1 (1990): 20.

8. Rebecca Sample Bernstein and Carolyn Torma, "Exploring the Role of Women in the Creation of Vernacular Architecture," in *Perspectives in Vernacular Architecture* 4, ed. Carter and Herman, 64–72.

9. Anders Grum, "Rendille Habitation," in Labelle Prussin, *African Nomadic Architecture: Space, Place, and Gender* (Washington, DC: Smithsonian Institution Press and National Museum of African Art, 1995), 163.

10. Shujaa Stories, "Women Builders of Mana: The Story of the Great Women Architects," produced in collaboration with Nature Kenya and National Museums of Kenya (Kenya, 2020), https://artsandculture.google.com/story/women-builders-of-mana-the-story-of-the-great-women-architects-national-museums-of-kenya/7AVBaaonrlblIQ?hl=en; Richard Beynon and Kelly Lilienfeld, "Ndebele Women," film produced by Shelagh Lubbock (New York: Filmakers Library, 1997).

11. Labelle Prussin, *African Nomadic Architecture: Space, Place, and Gender* (Washington, DC: Smithsonian Institution Press and National Museum of African Art, 1995).

12. Bernstein and Torma, "Exploring the Role of Women in the Creation of Vernacular Architecture."

13. Anna Pudianti, Lucia Asdra Rudiarti, and Vincentia Reni Vitasurya,

"Gender in the Transformation of Vernacular Architectural Settlements: Lessons from Brayut Rural Tourism, Yogyakarta, Indonesia," *Journal of the International Society for the Study of Vernacular Settlements* 7, no. 1 (January 2020): 39–48.

14. Carolyn Butler-Palmer, "Building Autonomy: A History of the Fifteenth Ward Hall of the Mormon Women's Relief Society," *Buildings and Landscapes* 20, no. 2 (Spring 2013): 69–94.

15. In the town of Ephraim, in 1881, the Relief Society owned a seven-acre silk farm, sheep, wheat, and co-op shares as well as their hall, and the home-manufactured goods they sold included cheese, eggs, carpet, cloth, and quilts. Thomas Carter, *Building Zion: The Material World of Mormon Settlements* (Minneapolis: University of Minnesota Press, 2015), 167.

16. Tania Martin, "The Mother House of the Grey Nuns: A Building History of the General Hospital," *JSSAC/JSÉAC* 24, no. 2 (1999): 40–49.

17. Tania Martin, "Housing the Grey Nuns: Power, Religion, and Women in fin-de-siècle Montréal," in *Perspectives in Vernacular Architecture 7: Exploring Everyday Landscapes*, ed. Annmarie Adams and Sally McMurry (Knoxville: University of Tennessee Press, 1997), 212–29.

18. Erin Cunningham, "Interiors, Histories, and the Preservation of Chicago's Hull House Settlement," *Buildings and Landscapes* 23, no. 2 (Fall 2016): 53–64.

19. Marta Gutman, *A City for Children: Women, Architecture, and the Charitable Landscapes of Oakland, 1850–1950* (Chicago: University of Chicago Press, 2014), 77–91

20. Daphne Spain, *Constructive Feminism: Women's Spaces and Women's Rights in the American City* (Ithaca: Cornell University Press, 2016), 56–57.

21. Spain, *Constructive Feminism*, 111–25.

22. By 1926, St. Vincent's explicitly only served White children. Gutman, *A City for Children*, 303.

23. Gutman, *A City for Children*, 298–320.

24. For example, Stella Nair found that, while women are not visible as contributing to Incan building in any of the secondary sources, primary documents describe women as among the builders and the patrons. Stella Nair, "Inca Ephemerality," (lecture at University of Virginia, Charlottesville, VA, December 7, 2023).

CHAPTER THREE

1. Roberta Gilchrist, *Gender and Material Culture: The Archaeology of Religious Women* (London: Routledge, 1994). See also Gabrielle Esperdy, "The Royal Abbey of Fontevrault: Religious Women and the Shaping of Gendered Space," *Journal of International Women's Studies* 6, no.2 (June 2005): 59–80.

2. Gilchrist, *Gender and Material Culture*, 124.

3. Abigail A. Van Slyck, "The Lady and the Library Loafer: Gender and Public Space in Victorian America," *Winterthur Portfolio* 31, no. 4 (Winter 1996): 221–42.

4. Amy G. Richter, *Home on the Rails: Women, the Railroad, and the Rise of Public Domesticity* (Chapel Hill: University of North Carolina Press, 2005).

5. Gail Bederman, *Manliness and Civilization: A Cultural History of Gender and Race in the United States, 1880–1917* (Chicago: University of Chicago Press, 1996).

6. William D. "The Masonic Lodge Room, 1870–1930: A Sacred Space of Masculine Spiritual Hierarchy," in *Perspectives in Vernacular Architecture* 5, ed. Cromley and Hudgins, 26–39: 35.

7. William D. Moore, *Masonic Temples: Freemasonry, Ritual Architecture, and Masculine Archetypes* (Knoxville: University of Tennessee Press, 2006); Moore, "The Masonic Lodge Room."

8. Moore, *Masonic Temples*, 20–27.

9. Paula Lupkin, *Manhood Factories: YMCA Architecture and the Making of Modern Urban Culture* (Minneapolis: University of Minnesota Press, 2010).

10. Lupkin, *Manhood Factories*.

11. Thomas Winter, *Making Men, Making Class: The YMCA and Workingmen, 1877–1920* (Chicago: University of Chicago Press, 2002).

12. Kautz Family YMCA Archives, "African Americans and the YMCA: Brief History," 2020, Archives and Special Collections, University of Minnesota Libraries, https://libguides.umn.edu/c.php?g=1088894&p=7940991. Julius Rosenwald also helped to fund the construction of nearly 5,000 public schools for Black students throughout the US South; Mary S. Hoffschwelle, *Preserving Rosenwald Schools* (Washington, DC: National Trust for Historic Preservation, 2012).

13. Carla Yanni, "The Coed's Predicament: The Martha Cook Building at the University of Michigan," *Buildings and Landscapes* 24, no. 1 (Spring 2017): 26–45; Carla Yanni, *Living on Campus: An Architectural History of the American Dormitory* (Minneapolis: University of Minnesota Press, 2019).

14. Helen Lefkowitz Horowitz, *Alma Mater: Design and Experience in the Women's Colleges from Their Nineteenth-Century Beginnings to the 1930s* (New York: Alfred A. Knopf, 1985), 69–133.

15. Horowitz, *Alma Mater*, 210–13.

16. Maureen A. Flanagan, *Constructing the Patriarchal City: Gender and the Built Environments of London, Dublin, Toronto, and Chicago, 1870s into the 1940s* (Philadelphia: Temple University Press, 2018); Harvey Molotch and Laura Nolan, eds., *Toilet: Public Restrooms and the Politics of Sharing* (New York: New York University Press, 2010); Barbara Penner, *Bathroom* (London: Reaktion Books, 2013); Joel Sanders, Susan Stryker, and Terry Kogan, *Stalled!* (website), accessed June 24, 2023, https://www.stalled.online/.

17. Elizabeth Yuko, "The Glamourous, Sexist History of the Women's Restroom Lounge," *Bloomberg CityLab*, Dec. 3, 2018, https://www.bloomberg.com/news/features/2018-12-03/the-rise-and-fall-of-the-women-s-restroom-lounge.

18. Angelique Chrisafis, "Protesters Damage 'Sexist' Open-Air Urinals in Paris: Uritrottoirs Seen as Discriminatory in City that Still Frowns on Breastfeeding," *The Guardian*, Aug. 29, 2018, https://www.theguardian.com/world/2018/aug/29/protesters-damage-sexist-open-air-urinals-in-paris.

19. Abigail A. Van Slyck, *A Manufactured Wilderness: Summer Camps and the Shaping of American Youth, 1890–1960* (Minneapolis: University of Minnesota Press, 2006), 159–66.

CHAPTER FOUR

1. Shirley Ardener, ed., *Women and Space: Ground Rules and Social Maps* (Providence: Berg, 1993), 3.

2. Henrietta L. Moore, *Space, Text, and Gender: An Anthropological Study of the Marakwet of Kenya* (New York: Guilford Press, 1996).

3. Francesca Bray, *Technology and Gender: Fabrics of Power in Late Imperial China* (Berkeley: University of California Press, 1997), 4.

4. Bray, *Technology and Gender*, 95.

5. Translated in Klaas Ruitenbeek, *Carpentry and Building in Late Imperial China: A Study of the Fifteenth-Century Carpenter's Manual Lu Ban Jing* (Leiden: E. J. Brill, 1993), 197.

6. Ruitenbeek, *Carpentry and Building in Late Imperial China*, 278.

7. Matrix, "House Design and Women's Roles," in *Making Space: Women and the Man-Made Environment* (London: Pluto Press, 1984), 55–80.

8. Bray, *Technology and Gender*; Rebecca Ginsburg, *At Home with Apartheid: The Hidden Landscapes of Domestic Service in Johannesburg* (Charlottesville: University of Virginia Press, 2011).

9. Leif Jerram, "Kitchen Sink Dramas: Women, Modernity and Space in Weimar Germany," *Cultural Geographies* 13, no. 4 (October 2006), 538–56.

10. Marion Roberts, *Living in a Man-Made World: Gender Assumptions in Modern Housing Design* (London: Routledge, 1991).

11. US Housing and Home Finance Agency, *Women's Congress on Housing* (Washington, DC: 1956), 3, 65–67, 77.

12. Dolores Hayden, *Redesigning the American Dream: The Future of Housing, Work, and Family Life* (New York: Norton, 1984). See also Dolores Hayden, *The Grand Domestic Revolution: A History of Feminist Designs for American Homes* (Cambridge, MA: MIT Press, 1981).

13. Penny Sparke, *As Long as It's Pink: The Sexual Politics of Taste* (London: Pandora, 1995) 194–203; Paoletti, *Pink and Blue*, 85-99.

14. Juliet Kinchin, "Interiors: Nineteenth-Century Essays on the 'Masculine'

and the 'Feminine' Room," in *The Gendered Object*, ed. Pat Kirkham (Manchester, UK: Manchester University Press, 1996), 12–29.

15. Hermann Muthesius, *Das Englische Haus* (Berlin: Wasmuth, 1904; English ed. New York: Rizzoli International, 1979), 206, quoted in Kinchin, 24.

16. On the expression of religion through decorative objects, see Colleen McDannell, *Material Christianity: Religion and Popular Culture in America* (New Haven: Yale University Press, 1995) and Kenneth Ames, "Words to Live By," and "When the Music Stops," in *Death in the Dining Room and Other Tales of Victorian Culture* (Philadelphia: Temple University Press, 1992). On comfort and the parlor, see Katherine C. Grier, *Culture and Comfort: Parlor Making and Middle-Class Identity* (Washington, DC: Smithsonian Books, 1988).

17. Ames, "Death in the Dining Room," in *Death and the Dining Room*, 44–96.

18. Grier, *Culture and Comfort.*

19. Thorstein Veblen, *The Theory of the Leisure Class: An Economic Study of Institutions* (London: Allen and Unwin, 1899), 70–73.

20. "Playboy's Penthouse Apartment: A Second Look at a High, Handsome Haven — Pre-planned and Furnished for the Bachelor in Town," *Playboy*, October 1956, 70.

21. Jessica Ellen Sewell, "Power, Sex, and Furniture: Masculinity and the Bachelor Pad in 1950s–60s America," Occasional Paper 43, School of Social Science, Institute for Advanced Study, Princeton, NJ, 2011.

22. Michelle Rosaldo, "Women, Culture, and Society: A Theoretical Overview," in *Women, Culture and Society*, ed. Michelle Zimbalist Rosaldo and Louise Lamphere (Stanford, CA: Stanford University Press, 1974), 17–42; Spain, *Gendered Spaces.*

23. US Bureau of Labor Statistics, "Household Data Annual Averages: 11. Employed Persons by Detailed Occupation, Sex, Race, and Hispanic or Latino Ethnicity," 2021, https://www.bls.gov/cps/cpsaat11.htm.

24. US Bureau of Labor Statistics, "Household Data Annual Averages."

25. In the early 1890s, Metropolitan Life, in New York City, staggered men's and women's start times and lunch breaks, and Metropolitan Life and multiple other corporations, including New England Mutual, Wells Fargo Nevada Bank, and Aetna, provided segregated lunchrooms and lounges. Angel Kwolek-Folland, *Engendering Business: Men and Women in the Corporate Office, 1870–1930* (Baltimore: Johns Hopkins University Press, 1994), 120–23.

26. US Bureau of Labor Statistics, "Household Data Annual Averages."

27. In 2021, 90% of receptionists and 96.4% of executive secretaries were female. US Bureau of Labor Statistics, "Household Data Annual Averages."

28. Kwolek-Folland, *Engendering Business*, 119.

29. Nikil Saval, "A Brief History of the Dreaded Office Cubicle," The Wall Street Journal, May 9, 2014. See also Nikil Saval, *Cubed: A Secret History of the Workplace.* New York: Doubleday, 2014.

30. Jürgen Habermas, *The Structural Transformation of the Public Sphere: An Inquiry into a Category of Bourgeois Society*, trans. Thomas Burger (Cambridge, MA: MIT Press, 1989), 33; Paul Freedman, "Women and Restaurants in the Nineteenth Century United States," *Journal of Social History* 48, no. 1 (2014): 1–19; Harvey A. Levenstein, *Revolution at the Table: The Transformation of the American Diet* (New York: Oxford University Press, 1988), 185.

31. Carolyn Brucken, "In the Public Eye: Women and the American Luxury Hotel," *Winterthur Portfolio* 31, no. 4 (1996): 203–20; Jessica Ellen Sewell, *Women and the Everyday City: Gender and Public Space in San Francisco, 1890–1915* (Minneapolis: University of Minnesota Press, 2011), 69–75.

32. Levenstein, *Revolution at the Table*, 185–90. *The Woman Who Waits*, by Frances R. Donovan (Boston: Richard G. Badger, 1920), provides a first-hand view of working in family restaurants in Chicago in the early twentieth century.

33. Sewell, *Women and the Everyday City*, 76–78.

34. Michael Batterberry and Ariane Batterberry, *On the Town in New York: The Landmark History of Eating, Drinking, and Entertainments from the American Revolution to the Food Revolution* (New York: Routledge, 1999), 145–47; Roy Rosenzweig, *Eight Hours for What We Will: Workers and Leisure in an Industrial City, 1870–1920* (Cambridge: Cambridge University Press, 1983), 63; Levenstein, *Revolution at the Table*, 185.

35. Sewell, *Women and the Everyday City*, 76–77; Levenstein, *Revolution at the Table*, 186.

36. Jane Stern and Michael Stern, "Cafeteria," *New Yorker*, August 1, 1988, 37–54; Batterberry and Batterberry, *On the Town in New York*, 187–89; Levenstein, *Revolution at the Table*, 187–88.

37. George Chauncey, *Gay New York: Gender, Urban Culture, and the Making of the Gay Male World, 1890–1940* (New York: Basic Books, 1994), 163–77.

38. Richard V. Francaviglia, *Main Street Revisited: Time, Space, and Image* (Iowa City: University of Iowa Press, 1996), 23–38.

39. Lisa Tolbert, "Commercial Blocks and Female Colleges: The Small-Town Business of Educating Ladies," in *Perspectives in Vernacular Architecture 6: Shaping Communities*, ed. Carter L. Hudgins and Elizabeth Collins Cromley (Knoxville: University of Tennessee Press, 1997), 204–15.

40. Sewell, *Women and the Everyday City*, xiv–xx; Jessica Sewell, "Sidewalks and Store Windows as Political Landscapes," in *Perspectives in Vernacular Architecture 9: Constructing Image, Identity, and Place*, ed. Alison K. Hoagland and Kenneth A. Breisch (Knoxville: University of Tennessee Press, 2003), 85–98.

CHAPTER FIVE

1. Doron Von Bieder, "From Rehovot," in *Queer Spaces: An Atlas of LGBTQ+ Places and Stories*, ed. Adam Nathaniel Furman and Joshua Mardell (London: RIBA, 2022), 50.

2. Important resources on queerness and domestic space include the special issue of *Home Cultures* 12, no.2 (2015) on "Alternative Sexualities," edited by Brent Pilkey, Rachel M. Scicluna, and Andrew Groman-Murray, as well as the collections Matt Cook, *Queer Domesticities: Homosexuality and Home Life in Twentieth-Century London* (New York: Palgrave Macmillan, 2014); and Brent Pilkey, Rachael M. Scicluna, Ben Campkin, and Barbara Penner, eds., *Sexuality and Gender at Home: Experience, Politics, Transgression* (London: Bloomsbury Academic, 2017)

3. Alice T. Friedman, "Hiding in Plain Sight: Love, Life and the Queering of Domesticity in Early Twentieth-Century New England," *Home Cultures* 12, no. 2 (2015): 139–67; Esther Newton, *Cherry Grove, Fire Island: Sixty Years in America's First Gay and Lesbian Town* (Durham, NC: Duke University Press, 2014).

4. Friedman, "Hiding in Plain Sight," 143; Annmarie Adams, "Sex and the Single Building: The Weston Havens House, 1941–2001," *Buildings and Landscapes* 17, no. 1 (2010): 82–97. A dramatic example of a queer house that shelters private space is the "Light Coffin" in Chiba, Japan, in which a radically open interior space is hidden by solid walls and can only be entered through a high shuttered window. See Alyssa Ueno, "Light Coffin–Dracula's Den," in *Queer Spaces*, ed. Furman and Mardell, 8–11.

5. Friedman, "Hiding in Plain Sight."

6. Henry Urbach, "Peeking at Gay Interiors," *Design Book Review* 25 (Summer 1992): 38.

7. Sarah A. Elwood, "Lesbian Living Spaces: Multiple Meanings of Home," *Journal of Lesbian Studies* 4, no. 1 (2000): 11–27.

8. Newton, *Cherry Grove*.

9. Fire Island Pines Historical Preservation Society, "The Archives," accessed May 1, 2023, https://www.pineshistory.org/the-archives/category/Architecture.

10. Elwood, "Lesbian Living Spaces."

11. Chauncey, *Gay New York*, 278–80; Lo Marshall, "Queer House Party," in *Queer Spaces*, ed. Furman and Mardell, 166–67.

12. Carla Barrett, "Queering the Home: The Domestic Labor of Lesbian and Gay Couples in Contemporary England," *Home Cultures* 12, no. 2 (2015): 193–211.

13. Tamar Rothenberg, "And She Told Two Friends: Lesbians Creating Urban Social Space," in *Mapping Desire*, ed. David Bell and Gill Valentine (London: Routledge, 1995), 165–81; Anne Enke, *Finding the Movement: Sexuality, Contested Space, and Feminist Activism* (Durham, NC: Duke University Press, 2007); Jen Jack Gieseking, *A Queer New York: Geographies of Lesbians, Dykes, and Queers* (New York: New York University Press, 2020); Susan Ferentinos, "Beyond the Bar: Properties Related to LGBTQ History," *Change Over Time* 8, no. 2 (Fall 2018): 148.

14. Genny Beemyn, *A Queer Capital: A History of Gay Life in Washington, D.C.* (New York: Routledge, 2015), 108–9.

15. Tim Retzloff, "Gay Organizing in the 'Desert of Suburbia' of Metropolitan Detroit," in *Making Suburbia: New Histories of Everyday America*, ed. John Archer, Paul J. P. Sandul, and Katherine Solomonson (Minneapolis: University of Minnesota Press, 2015), 51–62. The general membership meetings of the organization were held in commercial banquet rooms, as was fitting for an organization of largely professional White men who were interested in the politics of visibility.

16. Reina Gattusa, "How Lesbian Potlucks Nourished the LGBTQ Movement," *Atlas Obscura*, May 2, 2019, https://www.atlasobscura.com/articles/why-do-lesbians-have-potlucks-on-pride.

17. Rachel Scicluna, "Thinking Through Domestic Pluralities: Kitchen Stories from the Lives of Older Lesbians in London," *Home Cultures* 12, no. 2 (2015): 183.

18. On interior décor and queer identity, see John Potvin, *Bachelors of a Different Sort: Queer Aesthetics, Material Culture and the Modern Interior in Britain* (Manchester, UK: Manchester University Press, 2014); Brent Pilkey, "Reading the Queer Domestic Aesthetic Discourse: Tensions between Celebrated Stereotypes and Lived Realities," *Home Cultures* 12, no. 2 (2015): 213–39; and Andrew Gorman-Murray and Matt Cook, eds., *Queering the Interior* (London: Routledge, 2020).

19. Lynda Johnston and Gill Valentine, "Wherever I Lay My Girlfriend, That's My Home: The Performance and Surveillance of Lesbian Identities in Domestic Environments," in *Mapping Desire*, ed. Bell and Valentine, 99–113.

20. Kim D. Felsenthal, "Creating the Queendom: A Lens on Transy House," *Home Cultures* 6, no. 3 (2009): 243–60.

21. Alice T. Friedman, "Max Ewing's Closet and Queer Architectural History (Part 2)," *Platform*, October 21, 2021, https://www.platformspace.net/home/max-ewings-closet-and-queer-architectural-history-part-2.

22. Brent Pilkey, "Stepping into the Entrance Hallway: Glimpses of Public, Private and Personal Notions of the Self," in *Queering the Interior*, ed. Gorman-Murray and Cook, 37–48.

23. Elwood, "Lesbian Living Spaces."

24. On queer suburbia, see Julie A. Podmore and Alison L. Bain, "Whither Queer Suburbanisms? Beyond Heterosuburbia and Queer Metronormativities," *Progress in Human Geography* 45, no. 5 (2021): 1254–77; Retzloff, "Gay Organizing in the 'Desert of Suburbia'"; Karen Tongsten, *Relocations: Queer Suburban Imaginaries* (New York: New York University Press, 2011); Richard Phillips, Diane West, and David Shuttleton, *De-Centring Sexualities: Politics and Representation Beyond the Metropolis* (London: Routledge, 2000).

25. Paul Groth, *Living Downtown: The History of Residential Hotels in the United States* (Berkeley: University of California Press, 1994).

26. George Chauncey, "Lots of Friends at the YMCA: Rooming Houses, Cafeterias, and other Gay Social Centers," in *Gay New York*, 151–63.

27. Susan Stryker and Victor Silverman, dirs., *Screaming Queens: The Riot at Compton's Cafeteria*, KQED Truly CA, 2005 (14:30).

28. Facunda Revuelta, "Hotel Gondolín," in *Queer Spaces*, ed. Furman and Mardell.

29. Chauncey, *Gay New York*, 179–206.

30. Beemyn, *A Queer Capital*. Bars have also been important to White lesbian community, but lesbian bars are much rarer and thus have been less central to lesbian communities than bars have been to White gay men. See Gieseking, *A Queer New York*, and Enke, *Finding the Movement*. There are only 27 lesbian bars in the US in 2023, according to "The Lesbian Bar Project," accessed May 26, 2023, https://www.lesbianbarproject.com.

31. Jeremy Atherton Lin, *Gay Bar: Why We Went Out* (New York: Back Bay Books, 2021), 27.

32. Beemyn, *A Queer Capital*.

33. Henry Urbach, "Closets, Clothes, DisClosure," *Assemblage* 30 (1996): 62–73

34. Friedman, *Women and the Making of the Modern House*; Urbach, "Closets, Clothes, DisClosure"; Steven Cohan, "So Functional for its Purposes: The Bachelor Apartment in Pillow Talk," in *Stud: Architectures of* Masculinity, ed. Joel Sanders (New York: Princeton Architectural Press, 1996), 28–41; Michael P. Brown, *Closet Space: Geographies of Metaphor from the Body to the Globe* (New York: Routledge, 2000). For more on the idea of the closet, see Eve Kosofsky Sedgwick, *The Epistemology of the Closet* (Berkeley: University of California Press, 1990).

35. Barbara A. Weightman, "Gay Bars as Private Places," *Places* 24, no. 1 (1980): 11–12.

36. Lin, *Gay Bar*, 39.

37. Joan Nestle, "Restriction and Reclamation: Lesbian Bars and Beaches of the 1950s," in *Queers in Space: Communities, Public Places, Sites of Resistance*, ed. Gorden Brent Ingram, Anne-Marie Bouthillette, and Yolanda Retter (Seattle: Bay Press, 1997), 62.

38. Johan Andersson, "Hygiene Aesthetics on London's Gay Scene: The Stigma of AIDS," in *Dirt: New Geographies of Cleanliness and Contamination*, ed. Ben Campkin and Rosie Cox (London: Bloomsbury, 2012), 103.

39. Weightman, "Gay Bars," 14–16; Lin, *Gay Bar*; Nan Alamilla Boyd, *Wide-Open Town: A History of Queer San Francisco to 1965* (Berkeley: University of California Press, 2003), 126–27.

40. Joan Nestle, "Restriction and Reclamation," 62–63.

41. Nestle, Restriction and Reclamation." JD Samson, *Searching for the Last Lesbian Bars in America*, Broadly Specials, Vice Media Group, 2015.

42. Lin, *Gay Bar*, 96-7. See also Andersson, "Hygiene Aesthetics on London's Gay Scene."

43. Olivier Vallerand, *Homonormative Architecture and Queer Space: The Evolution of Gay Bars and Clubs in Montréal* (master's thesis, School of Architecture, McGill University, 2010).

44. Furman and Mardell, eds., *Queer Spaces*.

45. Kristen Hogan, *The Feminist Bookstore Movement: Lesbian Antiracism and Feminist Accountability* (Durham: Duke University Press, 2016).

46. ICI: A Woman's Place, letter, 1970, ICI: A Woman's Place Papers, Lesbian Herstory Archives, quoted in Hogan, *The Feminist Bookstore Movement*, 6.

47. Enke, *Finding the Movement*, 73.

48. Spencer Ackerman, "Two Pussy Riot Members Make Secret New York Appearance," *The Guardian*, June 5, 2013, https://www.theguardian.com/music/2013/jun/05/pussy-riot-members-unmask-new-york.

49. On coffeehouses see Enke, *Finding the Movement*. Ailo Ribas, "Train Journey," in *Queer Spaces*, ed. Furman and Mardell, 2–3, is an evocative exploration of transitory queer space, and other entries in the same book provide examples of temporarily queer-coded spaces.

50. Connie Harlan, interview, quoted in Enke, *Finding the Movement*, 145.

51. George Ross, *Tips on Tables: Being a Guide to Wining and Dining In New York* (New York: Covici-Friede, 1934), 238, and WPA (Federal Writers Project), *WPA Guide to New York City* (New York: Random House, 1939), 140, quoted in Chauncey, *Gay New York*, 167.

52. NYC LGBT Historic Sites Project, "Stewart's Cafeteria," accessed June 1, 2023, https://www.nyclgbtsites.org/site/stewarts-cafeteria/.

53. Stryker and Silverman, *Screaming Queens*.

54. Enke, *Finding the Movement*; Gieseking, *A Queer New York*; Hogan, *The Feminist Bookstore Movement*; Alex D. Ketchum, *Ingredients for Revolution: A History of American Feminist Restaurants, Cafes, and Coffeehouses* (Montreal: Concordia University Press, 2023). A work that pays some attention to spatiality and architecture is Spain, *Constructive Feminism*.

55. On historical shifts in sexual identities, see Jonathan Ned Katz, *The Invention of Heterosexuality* (New York: Dutton, 1995); John D'Emilio and Estelle B. Freedman, *Intimate Matters: A History of Sexuality in America* (Chicago: University of Chicago Press, 1997); Chauncy, *Gay New York*; and Siobhan Somerville, *Queering the Color Line: Race and the Invention of Heterosexuality in American Culture* (Durham: Duke University Press, 2000). The chapters in Regner Ramos and Sharif Mowlabocus, eds., *Queer Sites in Global Contexts: Technologies, Spaces, and Otherness* (London: Routledge, 2021) explore some of the multiplicities of queerness internationally, as do many of the entries in Furman and Mardell, eds., *Queer Spaces*.

CHAPTER SIX

1. Mary Jo Maynes and Ann Waltner, "Temporalities and Periodization in Deep History: Technology, Gender, and Benchmarks of 'Human Development,'" *Social Science History* 36, no. 1 (Spring 2012): 59–83.

2. Janet D. Spector, *What This Awl Means* (St. Paul: Minnesota Historical Society Press, 1993).

3. Whitney Battle-Baptiste, *Black Feminist Archaeology* (New York: Routledge, 2011), 87–107.

4. Sewell, *Women and the Everyday City*.

5. Alison Isenberg, *Downtown America: A History of the Place and the People* (Chicago: University of Chicago Press, 2005), 42–43.

6. Sewell, *Women and the Everyday City*, 75–84.

7. Stephen Vider, *The Queerness of Home: Gender, Sexuality and the Politics of Domesticity after World War II* (Chicago: University of Chicago Press, 2021), 18–19.

8. Friedman, "Max Ewing's Closet."

9. Lesbian Herstory Archives, *Our Herstory*, accessed June 9, 2023, https://lesbianherstoryarchives.org/about/a-brief-history/.

10. Deborah L. Rotman, *The Archaeology of Gender in Historic America* (Gainesville: University Press of Florida, 2015), 114–18.

11. Laurie Wilkie, *The Lost Boys of Zeta Psi: A Historical Archaeology of Masculinity at a University Fraternity* (Berkeley: University of California Press, 2010), 68–79.

12. Pamela Leong, "American Graffiti: Deconstructing Gendered Communication Patterns in Bathroom Stalls," *Gender, Place, and Culture* 23, no. 3 (January 2015): 306–27.

13. Sewell, *Women and the Everyday City*, xiv–xxii; 25–46.

14. Sewell, *Women and the Everyday City*, 6–24.

15. Abigail A. Van Slyck, *Free to All: Carnegie Libraries and American Culture, 1890–1920* (Chicago: University of Chicago Press, 1995); Van Slyck, *A Manufactured Wilderness*; Lupkin, *Manhood Factories*; Moore, *Masonic Temples*.

16. Sewell, *Women and the Everyday City*, 54–64.

17. Sarah Deutsch, *Women and the City: Gender, Space, and Power in New York, 1870–1940* (Oxford: Oxford University Press, 2000).

18. Chauncey, *Gay New York*.

19. Chauncey, *Gay New York*.

20. Annie Fader Haskell Diary, Haskell Family Papers, BANC MSS C-B 364, Bancroft Library, University of California, Berkeley.

21. Carter, *Building Zion*.

22. Chauncey, *Gay New York*, 58.

23. Lupkin, *Manhood Factories*, 102–9.

24. Horowitz, *Alma Mater*, 147–78.

25. Battle-Baptiste, *Black Feminist Archaeology*, 41–46.

26. Pamela Robertson Wojcik, *The Apartment Plot: Urban Living in American Film and Popular Culture, 1945 to 1975* (Durham NC: Duke University Press, 2010).

27. Spain, *Constructive Feminism*, 57.

28. Ephemeral sources like these are used for several of the entries in Furman and Mardell, eds., *Queer Spaces*.

29. See Sarah Pink, Kerstin Leder Mackley, Roxana Morosanu, Val Mitchell, and Tracy Bhamra, *Making Homes: Ethnography and Design* (New York: Routledge 2017); Esra Akcan, *Open Architecture: Migration, Citizenship, and the Urban Renewal of Berlin-Kreuzberg by IBA — 1984/87* (Basel: Birkhäuser, 2018), 36–38; Janina Gosseye, Naomi Stead, and Deborah van der Plaat, eds., *Speaking of Buildings: Oral History in Architectural Research* (New York: Princeton Architectural Press, 2019; and James Michael Buckley, "Just Fieldwork: Exploring the Vernacular in the African American Community in Portland Oregon's Albina District," *Future Anterior* 17, no. 2 (Winter 2020): 1–14.

30. Oral History Association, "Principles and Best Practices for Oral History," accessed June 20, 2023, https://oralhistory.org/about/principles-and-practices-revised-2009/.

31. A great resource for finding oral histories is Oral History Association, "Centers and Collections," accessed June 20, 2023, https://oralhistory.org/centers-and-collections/.

32. Brent Pilkey, "Stepping into the Entrance Hallway," in *Queering the Interior*, ed. Gorman-Murray and Cook, 37–48; David Brody, *Housekeeping by Design: Hotels and Labor* (Chicago: University of Chicago Press, 2016).

33. Annmarie Adams, "The Eichler Home: Intention and Experience in Postwar Suburbia," in *Perspectives in Vernacular Architecture* 5, ed. Cromley and Hudgins, 164–78.

34. Sarah Pink, *Home Truths: Gender, Domestic Objects and Everyday Life* (London: Routledge, 2004).

35. Andrew K. Sandoval-Strauss, "*Viewpoint*: Latino Vernaculars and the Emerging National Landscape," *Buildings and Landscapes* 10, no. 1 (Spring 2013); 1–18; Arijit Sen, "*Viewpoint*: Spatial Ethnography of Devon Avenue, Chicago," *Buildings and Landscapes* 28, no. 2 (Fall 2021), 3–24.

36. Arijit Sen, "Walking the Field in Milwaukee," *Platform*, July 13, 2020, https://www.platformspace.net/home/walking-the-field-in-milwaukee; "The Texas Freedom Colonies Project," directed by Andrea Roberts, accessed June 30, 2022. https://www.thetexasfreedomcoloniesproject.com/.

37. For an overview of this discourse, see Elizabeth Anderson, "Feminist Epistemology and Philosophy of Science," in *The Stanford Encyclopedia of Philosophy* (Spring 2020 Edition), ed. Edward N. Zalta, https://plato.stanford.edu/archives/spr2020/entries/feminism-epistemology/. For a discussion of

epistemology from an intersectional point of view, see Patricia Hill Collins, *Black Feminist Thought*.

38. Battle-Baptiste, *Black Feminist Archaeology*. For more on storytelling and vernacular architecture, see Ryan K. Smith, "*Viewpoint*: Building Stories; Narrative Prospects for Vernacular Architecture Studies," *Buildings and Landscapes* 12, no. 2 (Fall 2011): 1–14.

CONCLUSION

1. Sewell, *Women and the Everyday City*.

Bibliography

Ackerman, Spencer. "Two Pussy Riot Members Make Secret New York Appearance." *The Guardian*, June 5, 2013. https://www.theguardian.com/music/2013/jun/05/pussy-riot-members-unmask-new-york.

Adam, Peter. *Eileen Gray: Architect/Designer*. New York: Harry N. Abrams, 1987.

Adams, Annmarie. "The Eichler Home: Intention and Experience in Postwar Suburbia." In *Perspectives in Vernacular Architecture 5: Gender, Class, and* Culture, edited by Elizabeth Collins Cromley and Carter L. Hudgins, 164–78. Knoxville: University of Tennessee Press, 1995.

———. "Sex and the Single Building: The Weston Havens House, 1941–2001." *Buildings and Landscapes* 17, no. 1 (2010): 82–97.

Adams, Annmarie, and Sally McMurry, eds. *Perspectives in Vernacular Architecture 7: Exploring Everyday Landscapes*. Knoxville: University of Tennessee Press, 1997.

Agrest, Diana. *Architecture from Without: Framings for a Critical Practice*. Cambridge, MA: MIT Press, 1991.

Agrest, Diana, Patricia Conway, and Leslie Kanes Weisman, eds. *The Sex of Architecture*. New York: Harry N. Abrams, 1996.

Akcan, Esra. *Open Architecture: Migration, Citizenship, and the Urban Renewal of Berlin-Kreuzberg by IBA – 1984/87*. Basel, CH: Birkhäuser, 2018.

Ames, Kenneth. *Death in the Dining Room and Other Tales of Victorian Culture*. Philadelphia: Temple University Press, 1992.

Anderson, Elizabeth. "Feminist Epistemology and Philosophy of Science." In *The Stanford Encyclopedia of Philosophy* (Spring 2020 Edition), edited by Edward N. Zalta. https://plato.stanford.edu/archives/spr2020/entries/feminism-epistemology/.

Andersson, Johan. "Hygiene Aesthetics on London's Gay Scene: The Stigma of AIDS." In *Dirt: New Geographies of Cleanliness and Contamination*, edited by Ben Campkin and Rosie Cox, 103–12. London: Bloomsbury, 2012.

Andrzejewski, Anna. "*Perspectives in Vernacular Architecture*, the VAF and the Study of Ordinary Buildings and Landscapes in North America." *Perspectives in Vernacular Architecture* 13, no. 2 (2006–7): 55–63.

Archer, John, Paul J. P. Sandul, and Katherine Solomonson, eds., *Making Suburbia: New Histories of Everyday America*. Minneapolis: University of Minnesota Press, 2015.

Ardener, Shirley, ed. *Women and Space: Ground Rules and Social Maps*. Providence, RI: Berg, 1993.

Barker, Meg-John, and Jules Scheele. *Gender: A Graphic Guide*. London: Icon Books, 2019.

Barrett, Carla. "Queering the Home: The Domestic Labor of Lesbian and Gay Couples in Contemporary England." *Home Cultures* 12, no. 2 (2015): 193–211.

Batterberry, Michael, and Ariane Batterberry. *On the Town in New York: The Landmark History of Eating, Drinking, and Entertainments from the American Revolution to the Food Revolution*. New York: Routledge, 1999.

Battle-Baptiste, Whitney. *Black Feminist Archaeology*. New York: Routledge, 2011.

Bederman, Gail. *Manliness and Civilization: A Cultural History of Gender and Race in the United States, 1880–1917*. Chicago: University of Chicago Press, 1996.

Beemyn, Genny. *A Queer Capital: A History of Gay Life in Washington, D.C.* New York: Routledge, 2015.

Bell, David, and Gill Valentine, eds. *Mapping Desire: Geographies of Sexualities*. London: Routledge, 1995.

Berkeley, Ellen Perry, and Matilda McQuaid, eds. *Architecture: A Place for Women*. Washington, DC: Smithsonian Institution Press, 1989.

Bernstein, Rebecca Sample, and Carolyn Torma. "Exploring the Role of Women in the Creation of Vernacular Architecture." In *Perspectives in Vernacular Architecture 4*, edited by Thomas Carter and Bernard L. Herman, 64–72. Columbia: University of Missouri Press, 1991.

Beynon, Richard, and Kelly Lilienfeld. "Ndebele Women." Film produced by Shelagh Lubbock. New York: Filmakers Library, 1997.

Bloomer, Jennifer. "Big Jugs." In Arthur Kroker and Marilouise Kroker, eds., The Hysterical Male: New Feminist Theory, 13–27. London: Macmillan, 1991.

Bornstein, Kate. *My Gender Workbook: How to Become a Real Man, a Real Woman, the Real You, or Something Else Entirely*. New York: Routledge, 1998.

Boutelle, Sara Holmes. *Julia Morgan, Architect*. New York: Abbeville Press, 1995.

Boyd, Nan Alamilla. *Wide-Open Town: A History of Queer San Francisco to 1965*. Berkeley: University of California Press, 2003.

Boys, Jos, ed. *Disability, Space, Architecture: A Reader*. London: Routledge, 2017.

Bray, Francesca. *Technology and Gender: Fabrics of Power in Late Imperial China*. Berkeley: University of California Press, 1997.

Breisch, Kenneth A., and Alison K. Hoagland, eds. *Perspectives in Vernacular Architecture 10: Building Environments*. Knoxville: University of Tennessee Press, 2006.

Brody, David. *Housekeeping by Design: Hotels and Labor*. Chicago: University of Chicago Press, 2016.

Brown, James Benedict, Harriet Harriss, Ruth Morrow, and James Soane, eds.

A Gendered Profession: The Question of Representation in Space Making. London: RIBA, 2016.

Brown, Lori, and Karen Burns, eds. *Global Encyclopedia of Women in Architecture*. London: Bloomsbury, 2024.

Brown, Michael P. *Closet Space: Geographies of Metaphor from the Body to the Globe*. New York: Routledge, 2000.

Brucken, Carolyn. "In the Public Eye: Women and the American Luxury Hotel." *Winterthur Portfolio* 31, no. 4 (Winter 1996): 203–20.

Buckley, James Michael. "Just Fieldwork: Exploring the Vernacular in the African American Community in Portland Oregon's Albina District." *Future Anterior* 17, no. 2 (Winter 2020): 1–14.

Budd, Barbara, Pauline Rose Clance, and D. Emily Simerly. "Spatial Configurations: Erikson Reexamined." *Sex Roles* 12, no. 5/6 (1985): 571–77.

Butler, Judith. *Gender Trouble: Feminism and the Subversion of Identity*. New York: Routledge, 1990.

Butler-Palmer, Carolyn. "Building Autonomy: A History of the Fifteenth Ward Hall of the Mormon Women's Relief Society." *Buildings and Landscapes* 20, no. 2 (Spring 2013): 69–94.

Carter, Thomas. *Building Zion: The Material World of Mormon Settlements*. Minneapolis: University of Minnesota Press, 2015.

Carter, Thomas, and Elizabeth Collins Cromley. *Invitation to Vernacular Architecture: A Guide to the Study of Ordinary Buildings and Landscapes*. Knoxville: University of Tennessee Press, 2005.

Carter, Thomas, and Bernard L. Herman, eds. *Perspectives in Vernacular Architecture* 4. Columbia: University of Missouri Press, 1991.

Chauncey, George. *Gay New York: Gender, Urban Culture, and the Making of the Gay Male World, 1890–1940*. New York: Basic Books, 1994.

Chrisafis, Angelique. "Protesters Damage 'Sexist' Open-Air Urinals in Paris: Uritrottoirs Seen as Discriminatory in City that Still Frowns on Breastfeeding." *The Guardian*, August 29, 2018. https://www.theguardian.com/world/2018/aug/29/protesters-damage-sexist-open-air-urinals-in-paris.

Coleman, Debra, Elizabeth Danze, and Carol Henderson, eds. *Architecture and Feminism*. New York: Princeton Architectural Press, 1996.

Collins, Patricia Hill. *Black Feminist Thought: Knowledge, Consciousness, and the Politics of Empowerment*. New York: Routledge, 2000.

———. *Intersectionality as Critical Social Theory*. Durham, NC: Duke University Press, 2019.

Cook, Matt. *Queer Domesticities: Homosexuality and Home Life in Twentieth-Century London*. New York: Palgrave Macmillan, 2014.

Crenshaw, Kimberlé. *On Intersectionality: Essential Writings*. New York: New Press, 2017.

Cromley, Elizabeth Collins, and Carter L. Hudgins, eds. *Perspectives in Vernacular Architecture 5: Gender, Class, and Culture*. Knoxville: University of Tennessee Press, 1995.

Cunningham, Erin. "Interiors, Histories, and the Preservation of Chicago's Hull House Settlement." *Buildings and Landscapes* 23, no. 2 (Fall 2016): 53–64.

D'Emilio, John, and Estelle B. Freedman. *Intimate Matters: A History of Sexuality in America*. Chicago: University of Chicago Press, 1997.

Deutsch, Sarah. *Women and the City: Gender, Space, and Power in New York, 1870–1940*. Oxford: Oxford University Press, 2000.

Donovan, Frances R. *The Woman Who Waits*. Boston: Richard G. Badger, 1920.

Dreger, Alice. *Hermaphrodites and the Medical Invention of Sex*. Cambridge, MA: Harvard University Press, 2000.

Dubrow, Gail Lee, and Jennifer B. Goodman. *Restoring Women's History through Historic Preservation*. Baltimore: Johns Hopkins University Press, 2003.

Durning, Louise, and Richard Wrigley, eds. *Gender and Architecture*. Chichester, UK: Wiley, 2000.

Elwood, Sarah A. "Lesbian Living Spaces: Multiple Meanings of Home." *Journal of Lesbian Studies* 4, no. 1 (2000): 11–27.

Enke, Anne. *Finding the Movement: Sexuality, Contested Space, and Feminist Activism*. Durham, NC: Duke University Press, 2007.

Erikson, Erik. "Sex Differences in the Play Configurations of Preadolescents." *American Journal of Orthopsychiatry* 21 (1951): 667–93.

Esperdy, Gabrielle. "The Royal Abbey of Fontevrault: Religious Women and the Shaping of Gendered Space. *Journal of International Women's Studies* 6, no. 2 (June 2005): 59–80.

Felsenthal, Kim D. "Creating the Queendom: A Lens on Transy House." *Home Cultures* 6, no. 3 (2009): 243–60.

Ferentinos, Susan. "Beyond the Bar: Properties Related to LGBTQ History." *Change Over Time* 8, no. 2 (2018): 144–63.

Feuerstein, Marcia, Paula Zellner Bassett, and Jodi La Coe. *Expanding Field of Architecture: Women in Architecture Across the Globe*. London: Lund Humphries, 2022.

Fire Island Pines Historical Preservation Society. "The Archives." Accessed May 1, 2023, https://www.pineshistory.org/the-archives/category/Architecture.

Flanagan, Maureen A. *Constructing the Patriarchal City: Gender and the Built Environments of London, Dublin, Toronto, and Chicago, 1870s into the 1940s*. Philadelphia: Temple University Press, 2018.

Francaviglia, Richard V. *Main Street Revisited: Time, Space, and Image*. Iowa City: University of Iowa Press, 1996.

Freedman, Paul, "Women and Restaurants in the Nineteenth Century United States." *Journal of Social History* 48, no. 1 (2014): 1–19.

Frichot, Hélène, Catharina Gabrielsson, and Helen Bunting, eds. *Architecture and Feminisms: Ecologies, Economies, Technologies*. New York: Routledge, 2017.

Friedman, Alice T. "Hiding in Plain Sight: Love, Life and the Queering of Domesticity in Early Twentieth-Century New England." *Home Cultures* 12, no. 2 (2015): 139–67.

———. "Max Ewing's Closet and Queer Architectural History (Part 2)." *Platform*, October 21, 2021. https://www.platformspace.net/home/max-ewings-closet-and-queer-architectural-history-part-2.

———. *Women and the Making of the Modern House*. New Haven, CT: Yale University Press, 2007.

Furman, Adam Nathaniel, and Joshua Mardell, eds. *Queer Spaces: An Atlas of LGBTQIA+ Places and Stories*. London: RIBA, 2022.

Gattusa, Reina. "How Lesbian Potlucks Nourished the LGBTQ Movement," *Atlas Obscura*, May 2, 2019. https://www.atlasobscura.com/articles/why-do-lesbians-have-potlucks-on-pride.

Gieseking, Jen Jack. *A Queer New York: Geographies of Lesbians, Dykes, and Queers*. New York: New York University Press, 2020.

Gilchrist, Roberta. *Gender and Material Culture: The Archaeology of Religious Women*. London: Routledge, 1994.

Ginsburg, Rebecca. *At Home with Apartheid: The Hidden Landscapes of Domestic Service in Johannesburg*. Charlottesville: University of Virginia Press, 2011.

Gissen, David. *The Architecture of Disability: Buildings, Cities, and Landscapes beyond Access*. Minneapolis: University of Minnesota Press, 2022.

Glassie, Henry. *Folk Housing in Middle Virginia*. Knoxville: University of Tennessee Press, 1975.

———. "Meaningful Things and Appropriate Myths: The Artifact's Place in American Studies," *Prospects: An Annual of American Cultural Studies*, vol. 3 (October 1978), 1-49.

———. *Material Culture*. Bloomington: Indiana University Press, 1999.

Gordon, Michael, dir. *Pillow Talk*. Arwin Productions/Universal, 1959.

Gorman-Murray, Andrew, and Matt Cook, eds. *Queering the Interior*. New York: Routledge, 2018.

Gosseye, Janina, Naomi Stead, and Deborah van der Plaat, eds. *Speaking of Buildings: Oral History in Architectural Research*. New York: Princeton Architectural Press, 2019.

Grier, Katherine C. *Culture and Comfort: Parlor Making and Middle-Class Identity*. Washington, DC: Smithsonian Books, 1988.

Groth, Paul. *Living Downtown: The History of Residential Hotels in the United States*. Berkeley: University of California Press, 1994.

Gutman, Marta. *A City for Children: Women, Architecture, and the Charitable Landscapes of Oakland, 1850–1950*. Chicago: University of Chicago Press, 2014.

Gutman, Marta, and Ning de Coninck-Smith. *Designing Modern Childhoods: History, Space, and the Material Culture of Children*. New Brunswick, NJ: Rutgers University Press, 2008.

Habermas, Jürgen. *The Structural Transformation of the Public Sphere: An Inquiry into a Category of Bourgeois Society*. Translated by Thomas Burger. Cambridge, MA: MIT Press, 1989.

Hall, Jane. *Breaking Ground: Architecture by Women*. New York: Phaidon, 2019.

Hartman, Jan, ed. *The Women Who Changed Architecture*. New York: Princeton Architectural Press, 2022.

Haskell, Annie Fader. *Diary*. Haskell Family Papers. BANC MSS C-B 364, Bancroft Library, University of California, Berkeley

Hayden, Dolores. *The Grand Domestic Revolution: A History of Feminist Designs for American Homes*. Cambridge, MA: MIT Press, 1981.

———. *Redesigning the American Dream: The Future of Housing, Work, and Family Life*. New York: Norton, 1984.

Hoagland, Alison K., and Kenneth A. Breisch, eds. *Perspectives in Vernacular Architecture* 9*: Constructing Image, Identity, and Place*. Knoxville: University of Tennessee Press, 2003.

Hoffschwelle, Mary S. *Preserving Rosenwald Schools*. Washington, DC: National Trust for Historic Preservation, 2012.

Hofstra, Warren R., and Camille Wells. “Embracing Our Legacy, Shaping Our Future: The Vernacular Architecture Forum Turns Twenty-Five.” *Perspectives in Vernacular Architecture* 13, no. 2 (2006–7): 2–6.

Hogan, Kristen. *The Feminist Bookstore Movement: Lesbian Antiracism and Feminist Accountability*. Durham: Duke University Press, 2016.

Holdsworth, Deryck W. “‘I’m a Lumberjack and I’m OK’: The Built Environment and Varied Masculinities in the Industrial Age.” In Perspectives in Vernacular Architecture 5, Gender, Class, and Shelter, edited by Elizabeth Collins Cromley and Carter L. Hudgins, 11–25. Knoxville: University of Tennessee Press, 1995.

hooks, bell. *Ain’t I a Woman: Black Women and Feminism*. Boston: South End Press, 1981.

———. “Choosing the Margin as a Space of Radical Openness.” *Framework: The Journal of Cinema and Media* 36 (1989): 15–23.

Horowitz, Helen Lefkowitz. *Alma Mater: Design and Experience in the Women’s Colleges from Their Nineteenth-Century Beginnings to the 1930s*. New York: Alfred A. Knopf, 1985.

Hudgins, Carter L., and Elizabeth Collins Cromley, eds. *Perspectives in Vernacular Architecture* 6*: Shaping Communities*. Knoxville: University of Tennessee Press, 1997.

Hughes, Francesca, ed. *The Architect: Reconstructing Her Practice*. Cambridge, MA: MIT Press, 1996.

Ingram, Gordon Brent, Anne-Marie Bouthillette, and Yolanda Retter, eds.

Queers in Space: Communities, Public Places, Sites of Resistance. Seattle: Bay Press, 1997.

Isenberg, Alison. *Downtown America: A History of the Place and the People*. Chicago: University of Chicago Press, 2005.

James-Chakraborty, Kathleen. "Expanding Agency: Women and Modern Architecture and Design." Lecture at Yan P. Lin Centre, McGill University, February 21, 2022.

Jerram, Leif. "Kitchen Sink Dramas: Women, Modernity and Space in Weimar Germany." *Cultural Geographies* 13, no. 4 (October 2006): 538–56.

Jobst, Marko, and Naomi Stead, eds. *Queering Architecture: Methods, Practices, Pedagogies*. London: Bloomsbury, 2023.

Johnston, Lynda, and Gill Valentine. "Wherever I Lay My Girlfriend, That's My Home: The Performance and Surveillance of Lesbian Identities in Domestic Environments." In *Mapping Desire: Geographies of Sexualities*, edited by David Bell and Gill Valentine, 99–113. London: Routledge, 1995.

Katz, Jonathan Ned. *The Invention of Heterosexuality*. New York: Dutton, 1995.

Kautz Family YMCA Archives. "African Americans and the YMCA: Brief History." 2020. Archives and Special Collections, University of Minnesota Libraries. https://libguides.umn.edu/c.php?g=1088894&p=7940991.

Kessler, Suzanne J. *Lessons from the Intersexed*. New Brunswick, NJ: Rutgers University Press, 1998.

Ketchum Alex D. *Ingredients for Revolution: A History of American Feminist Restaurants, Cafes, and Coffeehouses*. Montreal: Concordia University Press, 2023.

Kirkham, Pat, ed. *The Gendered Object*. Manchester, UK: Manchester University Press, 1996.

Klee, Jeffrey E. "Viewpoint: Fieldwork, Mind, and Building." *Buildings and Landscapes* 25, no. 2 (Fall 2018): 1–16.

Kniffen, Fred B. "Folk Housing: Key to Diffusion." *Annals of the Association of American Geographers* 55 (1965): 549–77.

Kwolek-Folland, Angel. "Gender as a Category of Analysis in Vernacular Architecture Studies." In Perspectives in Vernacular Architecture 5: Gender, Class, and Shelter, edited by Elizabeth Collins Cromley and Carter L. Hudgins, 3–10. Knoxville: University of Tennessee Press, 1995.

———. *Engendering Business: Men and Women in the Corporate Office, 1870–1930*. Baltimore: Johns Hopkins University Press, 1994.

Leong, Pamela. "American Graffiti: Deconstructing Gendered Communication Patterns in Bathroom Stalls." *Gender, Place, and Culture* 23, no. 3 (January 2015): 306–27.

"The Lesbian Bar Project." Accessed May 26, 2023, https://www.lesbianbarproject.com.

Lesbian Herstory Archives. *Our Herstory*. Accessed June 9, 2023. https://lesbianherstoryarchives.org/about/a-brief-history/.

Levenstein, Harvey A. *Revolution at the Table: The Transformation of the American Diet.* New York: Oxford University Press, 1988.

Lewis, Pierce. "Axioms for Reading the Landscape: Some Guides to the American Scene," in *The Interpretation of Ordinary Landscapes: Geographical Essays*, edited by D. W. Meinig, 11–31. Oxford: Oxford University Press, 1979.

Lin, Jeremy Atherton. *Gay Bar: Why We Went Out.* New York: Back Bay Books, 2021.

Lupkin, Paula. *Manhood Factories: YMCA Architecture and the Making of Modern Urban Culture.* Minneapolis: University of Minnesota Press, 2010.

Making Room: Women and Architecture, Heresies 11, vol. 3, no. 3, 1981.

Marshall, Lo. "Queer House Party." In *Queer Spaces: An Atlas of LGBTQ+ Places and Stories*, edited by Adam Nathaniel Furman and Joshua Mardell, 166–67. London: RIBA, 2022.

Martin, Tania. "Housing the Grey Nuns: Power, Religion, and Women in fin-de-siècle Montréal." In *Perspectives in Vernacular Architecture 7: Exploring Everyday Landscapes*, edited by Annmarie Adams and Sally McMurry, 212-229. Knoxville: University of Tennessee Press, 1997.

———. "The Mother House of the Grey Nuns: A Building History of the General Hospital." *JSSAC/JSÉAC* 24, no. 2 (1999): 40–49.

Matrix. *Making Space: Women and the Man-Made Environment.* London: Pluto Press, 1984.

Maynes, Mary Jo, and Ann Waltner. "Temporalities and Periodization in Deep History: Technology, Gender, and Benchmarks of 'Human Development.'" *Social Science History* 36, no. 1 (Spring 2012): 59–83.

McCorquodale, Duncan, Katerina Ruedi, and Sarah Wigglesworth, eds. *Designing Practices: Architecture, Gender, and the Interdisciplinary.* London: Black Dog, 1996.

McDannell, Colleen. *Material Christianity: Religion and Popular Culture in America.* New Haven, CT: Yale University Press, 1995.

McMurry, Sally. "Women in the American Vernacular Landscape." *Material Culture* 20, no. 1 (Spring 1988): 33–49.

Meinig, D. W., ed. *The Interpretation of Ordinary Landscapes: Geographical Essays.* Oxford: Oxford University Press, 1979.

Miller, Marla R. "Labor and Liberty in the Age of Refinement: Gender, Class, and the Built Environment." In *Perspectives in Vernacular Architecture* 10: Building Environments, edited by Kenneth A. Breisch and Alison K. Hoagland, 15-31. Knoxville: University of Tennessee Press, 2006.

Molotch, Harvey, and Laura Nolan, eds., *Toilet: Public Restrooms and the Politics of Sharing.* New York: New York University Press, 2010.

Moore, Henrietta L. *Space, Text, and Gender: An Anthropological Study of the Marakwet of Kenya.* New York: Guilford Press, 1996.

Moore, William D. "The Masonic Lodge Room, 1870-1930: A Sacred Space of

Masculine Spiritual Hierarchy." In *Perspectives in Vernacular Architecture 5: Gender, Class, and Shelter*, edited by Elizabeth Collins Cromley and Carter L. Hudgins, 26-39. Knoxville: University of Tennessee Press, 1995.

———. *Masonic Temples: Freemasonry, Ritual Architecture, and Masculine Archetypes*. Knoxville: University of Tennessee Press, 2006.

Nair, Stella. "Inca Ephemerality." Lecture at University of Virginia, Charlottesville, VA, December 7, 2023.

Nestle, Joan. "Restriction and Reclamation: Lesbian Bars and Beaches of the 1950s." In *Queers in Space: Communities, Public Places, Sites of Resistance*, edited by Gorden Brent Ingram, Anne-Marie Bouthillette, and Yolanda Retter, 61–67. Seattle: Bay Press, 1997,

Newton, Esther. *Cherry Grove, Fire Island: Sixty Years in America's First Gay and Lesbian Town*. Durham, NC: Duke University Press, 2014.

Oral History Association. "Principles and Best Practices for Oral History." Accessed June 20, 2023. https://oralhistory.org/about/principles-and-practices-revised-2009.

Paoletti, Jo B. *Pink and Blue: Telling the Boys from the Girls in America*. Bloomington: Indiana University Press, 2012.

Penner, Barbara. *Bathroom*. London: Reaktion Books, 2013.

Phillips, Richard, Diane West, and David Shuttleton, eds. *De-Centering Sexualities: Politics and Representation beyond the Metropolis*. London: Routledge, 2000.

Pilkey, Brent. "Reading the Queer Domestic Aesthetic Discourse: Tensions between Celebrated Stereotypes and Lived Realities." *Home Cultures* 12, no. 2 (2015): 213–39.

Pilkey, Brent. "Stepping into the Entrance Hallway: Glimpses of Public, Private and Personal Notions of the Self." In *Queering the Interior*, edited by Andrew Gorman-Murray and Matt Cook, 37-48. New York and London: Routledge, 2018.

Pilkey, Brent, Rachael M. Scicluna, Ben Campkin, and Barbara Penner, eds. *Sexuality and Gender at Home: Experience, Politics, Transgression*. London: Bloomsbury Academic, 2017.

Pilkey, Brent, Rachael M. Scicluna, and Andrew Gorman-Murray, eds. "Alternative Domesticities: A Cross-Disciplinary Approach to Home and Sexuality." Special Issue, *Home Cultures* 12, no. 2 (2015).

Pink, Sarah. *Home Truths: Gender, Domestic Objects and Everyday Life*. London: Routledge, 2004.

Pink, Sarah, Kerstin Leder Mackley, Roxana Morosanu, Val Mitchell, and Tracy Bhamra. *Making Homes: Ethnography and Design*. New York: Routledge, 2017.

"Playboy's Penthouse Apartment: A Second Look at a High, Handsome Haven — Pre-planned and Furnished for the Bachelor in Town." *Playboy*, October 1956, 65–70.

Podmore, Julie A., and Alison L. Bain. "Whither Queer Suburbanisms? Beyond Heterosuburbia and Queer Metronormativities." *Progress in Human Geography* 45, no. 5 (2021): 1254–77.

Potvin, John. *Bachelors of a Different Sort: Queer Aesthetics, Material Culture and the Modern Interior in Britain*. Manchester, UK: Manchester University Press, 2014.

Prown, Jules David. "Mind in Matter: An Introduction to Material Culture Theory and Method." *Winterthur Portfolio* 17, no. 1 (Spring 1982): 1–19.

Prussin, Labelle. *African Nomadic Architecture: Space, Place, and Gender*. Washington, DC: Smithsonian Institution Press and National Museum of African Art, 1995.

Pudianti, Anna, Lucia Asdra Rudiarti, and Vincentia Reni Vitasurya, "Gender in the Transformation of Vernacular Architectural Settlements: Lessons from Brayut Rural Tourism, Yogyakarta, Indonesia." *Journal of the International Society for the Study of Vernacular Settlements* 7, no. 1 (January 2020): 39–48.

Ramos, Regner, and Sharif Mowlabocus, eds. *Queer Sites in Global Contexts: Technologies, Spaces, and Otherness*. London: Routledge, 2021.

Rendell, Jane, Barbara Penner, and Iain Borden, eds. *Gender Space Architecture: An Interdisciplinary Introduction*. New York: Routledge, 2000.

Retzloff, Tim. "Gay Organizing in the 'Desert of Suburbia' of Metropolitan Detroit." In *Making Suburbia: New Histories of Everyday America*, edited by John Archer, Paul J. P. Sandul, and Katherine Solomonson, 51– 62. Minneapolis: University of Minnesota Press, 215.

Revuelta, Facunda. "Hotel Gondolín," In *Queer Spaces: An Atlas of LGBTQIA+ Places and Stories*, edited by Adam Nathaniel Furman and Joshua Mardell, 28–29. London: RIBA, 2022.

Ribas, Ailo. "Train Journey." In *Queer Spaces: An Atlas of LGBTQIA+ Places and Stories*, edited by Adam Nathaniel Furman and Joshua Mardell, 2–3. London: RIBA, 2022.

Richter, Amy G. *Home on the Rails: Women, the Railroad, and the Rise of Public Domesticity*. Chapel Hill: University of North Carolina Press, 2005.

Roberts, Marion. *Living in a Man-Made World: Gender Assumptions in Modern Housing Design*. London: Routledge, 1991.

Rosaldo, Michelle Zimbalist, and Louise Lamphere, eds. *Women, Culture and Society*. Stanford, CA: Stanford University Press, 1974.

Rosenzweig, Roy. *Eight Hours for What We Will: Workers and Leisure in an Industrial City, 1870–1920*. Cambridge: Cambridge University Press, 1983.

Rothenberg, Tamar. "And She Told Two Friends: Lesbians Creating Urban Social Space." In *Mapping Desire*, edited by David Bell and Gill Valentine, 165-81. London: Routledge, 1995.

Rotman, Deborah L. *The Archaeology of Gender in Historic America*. Gainesville: University Press of Florida, 2015.

Rotman, Deborah L., and Ellen-Rose Savulis. *Shared Spaces and Divided Places: Material Dimensions of Gender Relations and the American Historical Landscape.* Knoxville: University of Tennessee Press, 2003.

Ruitenbeek, Klaas. *Carpentry and Building in Late Imperial China: A Study of the Fifteenth-Century Carpenter's Manual Lu Ban Jing.* Leiden, NL: E. J. Brill, 1993.

Salzman, Jack, ed. Prospects: An Annual of American Cultural Studies, vol. 3. New York: Burt Franklin, 1978.

Samson, JD. *Searching for the Last Lesbian Bars in America.* Broadly Specials, Vice Media Group, 2015.

Sanders, Joel, ed. *Stud: Architectures of Masculinity.* New York: Princeton Architectural Press, 1996.

Sanders, Joel, Susan Stryker, and Terry Kogan. *Stalled!* (website). Accessed June 24, 2023, https://www.stalled.online/.

Sandoval-Strauss, Andrew K. "*Viewpoint*: Latino Vernaculars and the Emerging National Landscape." *Buildings and Landscapes* 20, no. 1 (Spring 2013): 1–18.

Saval, Nikil. "A Brief History of the Dreaded Office Cubicle." *The Wall Street Journal*, May 9, 2014.

———. *Cubed: A Secret History of the Workplace.* New York: Doubleday, 2014.

Schwitalla, Ursula, ed. *Women in Architecture: Past, Present, and Future.* Berlin: Hatje Cantz Verlag, 2021.

Scicluna, Rachel. "Thinking Through Domestic Pluralities: Kitchen Stories from the Lives of Older Lesbians in London." *Home Cultures* 12, no. 2 (2015): 169–91.

Scott, Joan Wallach. "Gender: A Useful Category of Social Analysis." *American Historical Review* 91, no. 5 (1986): 1053–75.

Sedgwick, Eve Kosofsky. *The Epistemology of the Closet.* Berkeley: University of California Press, 1990.

Sen, Arijit. "*Viewpoint*: Spatial Ethnography of Devon Avenue, Chicago." *Buildings and Landscapes* 28, no. 2 (Fall 2021): 3–24.

———. "Walking the Field in Milwaukee." *Platform*, July 13, 2020. https://www.platformspace.net/home/walking-the-field-in-milwaukee.

Sewell, Jessica Ellen. "Sidewalks and Store Windows as Political Landscapes." In *Perspectives in Vernacular Architecture 9: Constructing Image, Identity, and Place*, edited by Alison K. Hoagland and Kenneth A. Breisch, 85–98. Knoxville: University of Tennessee Press, 2003.

———. "Power, Sex, and Furniture: Masculinity and the Bachelor Pad in 1950s–60s America." Occasional Paper 43, School of Social Science, Institute for Advanced Study, Princeton, NJ, 2011.

———. *Women and the Everyday City: Gender and Public Space in San Francisco, 1890–1915.* Minneapolis: University of Minnesota Press, 2011.

Shakespeare, Tom. "Disabled Sexuality: Toward Rights and Recognition." *Sexuality and Disability* 18, no. 3 (2000).

Shujaa Stories. "Women Builders of Mana: The Story of the Great Women Architects." Produced in collaboration with Nature Kenya and National Museums of Kenya. Kenya, 2020. https://artsandculture.google.com/story/JAJCaaonrlblIQ.

Smith, Ryan K. "*Viewpoint*: Building Stories: Narrative Prospects for Vernacular Architecture Studies." *Buildings and Landscapes* 12, no. 2 (Fall 2011): 1–14.

Sokolina, Anna, ed. *The Routledge Companion to Women in Architecture*. London: Routledge, 2024.

Somerville, Siobhan. *Queering the Color Line: Race and the Invention of Heterosexuality in American Culture*. Durham, NC: Duke University Press, 2000.

Spain, Daphne. *Constructive Feminism: Women's Spaces and Women's Rights in the American City*. Ithaca, NY: Cornell University Press, 2016.

———. *Gendered Spaces*. Chapel Hill: University of North Carolina Press, 1992.

Sparke, Penny. *As Long as It's Pink: The Sexual Politics of Taste*. London: Pandora, 1995.

Spector, Janet D. *What This Awl Means*. St. Paul: Minnesota Historical Society Press, 1993.

Stern, Jane, and Michael Stern. "Cafeteria." *New Yorker*, August 1, 1988, 37–54

Stryker, Susan, and Victor Silverman, dirs. *Screaming Queens: The Riot at Compton's Cafeteria*. KQED Truly CA, 2005.

Swentzell, Rina. "Conflicting Landscape Values: The Santa Clara Pueblo and Day School." *Places* 7, no. 1 (1990): 19–27.

"The Texas Freedom Colonies Project." Directed by Andrea Roberts. Accessed June 20, 2022. https://www.thetexasfreedomcoloniesproject.com/.

Thorpe, Richard, dir. *That Funny Feeling*. Universal Pictures, 1965.

Tolbert, Lisa. "Commercial Blocks and Female Colleges: The Small-Town Business of Educating Ladies." In *Perspectives in Vernacular Architecture* 6, *Shaping Communities*, edited by Carter L. Hudgins and Elizabeth Collins Cromley, 204–15. Knoxville: University of Tennessee Press, 1997.

Tongsten, Karen. *Relocations: Queer Suburban Imaginaries*. New York: New York University Press, 2011.

Torre, Susanna, ed. *Women in American Architecture: A Historic and Contemporary Perspective*. New York: Whitney Library of Design, 1977.

Truth, Sojourner. "Ain't I a Woman?" Speech delivered to the Women's Convention, Akron, Ohio, 1851. Modern History Sourcebook, Fordham University, https://sourcebooks.fordham.edu/mod/sojtruth-woman.asp.

Ueno, Alyssa. "Light Coffin–Dracula's Den." In *Queer Spaces: An Atlas of LGBTQ+ Places and Stories*, edited by Adam Nathaniel Furman and Joshua Mardell, 8–11. London: RIBA, 2022.

Upton, Dell. "The VAF at 25: What Now?" *Perspectives in Vernacular Architecture* 13, no. 2 (2006–7): 7–13.

Upton, Dell, and John Michael Vlach, eds., *Common Places: Readings in American Vernacular Architecture*. Athens: University of Georgia Press, 1986.

Urbach, Henry. "Closets, Clothes, DisClosure." *Assemblage* 30 (1996): 62–73.

———. "Peeking at Gay Interiors." *Design Book Review* 25 (Summer 1992): 38–40.

US Bureau of Labor Statistics. "Household Data Annual Averages: 11. Employed Persons by Detailed Occupation, Sex, Race, and Hispanic or Latino Ethnicity." Washington, DC, 2021. https://www.bls.gov/cps/cpsaat11.htm.

US Housing and Home Finance Agency. *Women's Congress on Housing*. Washington, DC, 1956.

Vallerand, Olivier. *Homonormative Architecture and Queer Space: The Evolution of Gay Bars and Clubs in Montréal*. Master's thesis, School of Architecture, McGill University, 2010.

Van Slyck, Abigail A. *Free to All: Carnegie Libraries and American Culture, 1890–1920*. Chicago: University of Chicago Press, 1995.

———. "The Lady and the Library Loafer: Gender and Public Space in Victorian America." *Winterthur Portfolio* 31, no. 4 (Winter 1996): 221–42.

———. *A Manufactured Wilderness: Summer Camps and the Shaping of American Youth, 1890–1960*. Minneapolis: University of Minnesota Press, 2006.

Veblen, Thorstein. *The Theory of the Leisure Class: An Economic Study in the Evolution of Institutions*. New York: Macmillan, 1899.

Vider, Stephen. *The Queerness of Home: Gender, Sexuality and the Politics of Domesticity after World War II*. Chicago: University of Chicago Press, 2021.

Vlach, John. "The Shotgun House: An African Architectural Legacy: Part One." *Pioneer America* 8, no. 1 (January 1976): 47–60.

———. "The Shotgun House: An African Architectural Legacy: Part Two." *Pioneer America* 8, no. 2 (July 1976): 57–70.

Von Bieder, Doron. "From Rehovot." In *Queer Spaces: An Atlas of LGBTQ+ Places and Stories*, edited by Adam Nathaniel Furman and Joshua Mardell, 50. London: RIBA, 2022.

Wall, Diana diZerega. *The Archaeology of Gender: Separating the Spheres in Early America*. New York: Springer, 1994.

Weightman, Barbara A. "Gay Bars as Private Places." *Places* 24, no. 1 (1980): 9–16.

Weiner, Annette. *Women of Value; Men of Renown: New Perspectives in Trobriand Exchange*. Austin: University of Texas Press, 1976.

Wells, Camille, ed. *Perspectives in Vernacular Architecture* 1. Columbia: University of Missouri Press, 1982.

———, ed. *Perspectives in Vernacular Architecture* 2. Columbia: University of Missouri Press, 1986.

———. "Old Claims and New Demands: Vernacular Architecture Studies Today." In *Perspectives in Vernacular Architecture* 2, edited by Camile Wells, 1–10. Columbia: University of Missouri Press, 1986.

Wilkie, Laurie. *The Lost Boys of Zeta Psi: A Historical Archaeology of Masculinity at a University Fraternity*. Berkeley: University of California Press, 2010.

Wilson, Chris, and Paul Groth, eds. *Everyday America: Cultural Landscape Studies after J. B. Jackson*. Berkeley: University of California Press, 2003.

Winter, Thomas. *Making Men, Making Class: The YMCA and Workingmen, 1877–1920*. Chicago: University of Chicago Press, 2002.

Wojcik, Pamela Robertson. *The Apartment Plot: Urban Living in American Film and Popular Culture, 1945 to 1975*. Durham, NC: Duke University Press, 2010.

Yanni, Carla. "The Coed's Predicament: The Martha Cook Building at the University of Michigan." *Buildings and Landscapes* 24, no. 1 (Spring 2017): 26–45.

———. *Living on Campus: An Architectural History of the American Dormitory*. Minneapolis: University of Minnesota Press, 2019.

Young, Iris Marion. "Throwing Like a Girl: A Phenomenology of Feminine Body Comportment Motility and Spatiality." *Human Studies* 3 (1980): 137–56.

Yuko, Elizabeth. "The Glamourous, Sexist History of the Women's Restroom Lounge." *Bloomberg CityLab*, Dec. 3, 2018, https://www.bloomberg.com/news/features/2018-12-03/the-rise-and-fall-of-the-women-s-restroom-lounge.

Index

Entries in bold refer to illustrations

www.ingramcontent.com/pod-product-compliance
Lightning Source LLC
LaVergne TN
LVHW081755060925
820435LV00020B/176

* 9 7 8 1 6 2 1 9 0 9 3 1 6 *